"The Chic Entrepreneur offers invaluable advice to women on how to use every wile available to create a highly profitable business. The Chic Entrepreneur is engaging, intelligent and practical not to mention fun to read. If you are interested in building a business properly, in order to achieve not only financial freedom but personal freedom as well, this is the book for you."

Gail Evans, Author of the New York Times Bestseller
Play Like a Man, Win Like a Woman

"Finally a business book that speaks directly to women. Elizabeth Gordon delivers an insightful method for building a company for women who want to succeed with style."

Delia Passi, CEO & President of MedeliaCommunications,
Author of Winning the Toughest Customer:
The Essential Guide to Selling to Women

"This book gives you a proven formula for thinking and acting to build a fast-growing, profitable business in any market."

Brian Tracy, Author of The Way to Wealth

"A delightful read for entrepreneurs who want to build their businesses with style!"

Cynthia Good, Founding Editor & CEO PINKmagazine

"It is never too late to be reminded of valuable business techniques and success traits. Elizabeth Go----- ----- ----- and on target with The Chic Entrepreneur. Th---- ----- ----- ----- ntent summaries and short cut rem----- ----- ----- being entrepreneurs. This is an inval----- ----- ----- neur in the making. I certainly wish this had b---- ----- ----- umped into the wild blue yonder of business ownership more than a decade ago. It would have made the journey smoother. "

Melissa Galt, America's Lifestyle Diva
Author of Celebrate Your Life!
National motivational speaker and successful entrepreneur

"Elizabeth Gordon is a genius! I barely got through the first few pages before I realized that I better get out a pen and paper to take notes. Sometimes we business savvy gals think we know it all — but a fresh perspective and dead-on advice is so critical to our success. I especially loved the Chic Tips offered on particular pages to capsule significant actions or mindset changes. I'll be recommending The Chic Entrepreneur to my clients and workshop participants. It's that good!"

Mary Kurek, Speaker/Networking & Marketing Expert
Author of Who's Hiding in Your Address Book —
Introducing the Ideal Network for Successful Women

The Chic Entrepreneur

Put Your Business in Higher Heels

Elizabeth W. Gordon
with Leanna Adams

Robert D. Reed Publishers
P.O. Box 1992
Bandon, OR 97411
Phone: 541-347-9882; Fax: -9883
E-mail: 4bobreed@msn.com
Website: www.rdrpublishers.com

Editors: Susan Carr and Barbara Harrison
Cover Designer: Cleone Lyvonne
Typesetter: Mait Ainsaar, BICN Marketing & Design

ISBN: 978-1-934759-04-2

Library of Congress Control Number: 2007943459

Manufactured, Typeset, and Printed in the United States of America

ACKNOWLEDGMENTS

We would like to thank our parents, Arlene and Walt Gordon and Virginia and Jay Adams, for giving us the encouragement to dream big dreams and the smarts and savvy to achieve them; our fiancés, Stephen Minshaw and George Leach, for their hugs and kisses and unyielding emotional support; and our friends (thankfully there are too many to name) for keeping us in good humor along the way.

A huge thank you goes to Susan Carr for her thorough editing, fabulous suggestions, and her boundless enthusiasm for this and all of our projects. We are so happy to have you on the Chic Team.

Thanks to our visionary publisher, Bob Reed, for giving us the idea for the book and the support to make the project a success, and his lovely sidekick, Cleone Lyvonne, for the fabulous cover design and sales support.

Lastly, we'd like to thank each other for making this book possible. We've created something greater together than either of us ever could have apart. Teamwork led by vision is a beautiful thing.

TABLE OF CONTENTS

Introduction

Any woman can be an entrepreneur. Working as a business consultant for more than a decade has taught me this. However, if you want to be a Chic Entrepreneur, you have to combine style with industriousness. Being chic is about how you carry yourself and the choices you make. It's not about the clothes you wear or the way you cut your hair; it's about your attitude and your actions. Chic Entrepreneurs balance optimism with realism; they know who they are, and they know where they are going. A Chic Entrepreneur knows the future is bright and has many great things in store for her, so she dresses like the leader of the business she wants, not the worker bee in the business that she has. Being chic is not about being perfect; it's about being you at your best. A Chic Entrepreneur knows when to persevere and when to cut her losses. She sees the big picture and knows her role in it. She understands that a business is a living organism, with great potential for growth if tended to properly. A Chic Entrepreneur is not interested in a get-rich-quick scheme. She realizes that she will reap what she sows, so she takes the time to learn how to build a business right. Being chic is about being professional, having integrity, never burning bridges, and working hard, but more importantly, working smart. Chic Entrepreneurs are a rare and powerful breed. They realize they are in charge of their lives. Rather than waiting for something to happen, they make it happen. These women tend to be in the ten percent of startup businesses that actually succeed. Why, you ask? Because a Chic Entrepreneur knows what she's doing and she acts like it. She understands that business is about risk and return; she handles the risks and enjoys the returns. Chic Entrepreneurs know that to be successful in today's tough business climate they have to provide unique value to the market, have a strategic plan, wow customers, inspire employees, ante up the necessary startup costs, and turn those costs into a waterfall of cash flow.

You can be a Chic Entrepreneur, too. You can even start in your spare time. Everyone has to start somewhere, right? I started down the path of entrepreneurship the summer after my freshman year in college, selling high-end knives to housewives when I wasn't working my day job. Not a particularly glamorous or novel venture, but an invaluable experience for a budding businesswoman. This venture enabled me to buy my first car, and it endowed me with many entrepreneurial essentials like fronting an investment in order to sell something I believed in, cold calling, setting my own schedule, focusing on the customer, asking for referrals, overcoming objections, and dealing with defeat, along with teamwork, leadership, and self-motivation. I also learned how good it felt to win and how fun it was to have the freedom to do it my way.

If you truly want to be a Chic Entrepreneur, you'll need to start with a good business idea, but realize that is only the beginning. Your idea must be both viable and unique. Business is all about providing unique value to the marketplace. When you're able to

the idea is only the beginning 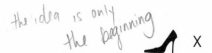 X

create or source your value at a cost lower than the price you can sell it for (less all of your other fixed expenses), you earn profit—which you can take to the bank...or the mall. Making sure that your business idea is unique requires research and creativity. Executing that unique idea takes *boldness and *persistence. Chic Entrepreneurs are not afraid to be themselves. They see their uniqueness as empowering instead of hampering, and they dare to be different. They also realize that success does not come overnight; it comes over time, after learning but not before making some mistakes.

Once you've had your flash of brilliance, the next necessary step in becoming a Chic Entrepreneur is forming an actual business. You are not an entrepreneur if you just have an idea and are sitting on it. There are dreamers and doers in this world and the Chic Entrepreneur is both. She dreams of what could be and then she gets off her behind and makes it happen.

That's what this book is all about. It's about *how* to turn your business dreams into a chic reality. Having the idea is just the first step. You need to translate that idea into true marketable value, and then build a profitable business model around it. If you haven't taken the leap yet, this book will get you prepared to and excited about diving in. If you are already swimming in entrepreneurial waters, this book will help you to refine your stroke so you can cruise along freestyle instead of simply splashing about or tiredly treading water.

The path to Chic Entrepreneurship takes a road map. You certainly don't want to wander around the city in high heels not knowing where you are going. You need a strategy. Fortunately, you are now holding in your hands your map to achieving chic success. Putting your business in higher heels means making it more successful and making it more attractive to others. Of course, being in higher heels is not always the most comfortable experience, but in order to grow and achieve greater things, you have to step outside of your comfort zone. Building a business is a journey during which you need to be open to trying new things and taking risks. You must be willing to stumble, and even fall, in order to succeed.

Becoming a Chic Entrepreneur is a lifetime pursuit and oftentimes a challenging one, but take it from me, it's worth the hard work, because in just a few years you'll be sitting pretty with a business you love and the lifestyle you desire.

Now, let's get started.

CHAPTER ONE

Payless or Nordstrom: What's Your Value?

Payless and Nordstrom are two companies known for their shoes. Some people say Payless is where you get the most value for your money: You can easily buy three pairs of cute shoes for less than the price of dinner at a fancy-pants restaurant. Quantity is one measure of value, and when you've got three new outfits to accessorize and a shoestring budget for matching footwear, this is the kind of value you need. Of course, when you get invited to go to that fancy-pants restaurant, you might not feel comfortable wearing your Payless pumps. At that point, you'll probably head on over to super swanky Nordstrom where you can buy shoes that will look fabulous from near and far, feel comfortable all night long because they are carefully crafted with real leather and other expensive materials, and last for more than one season.

At Nordstrom, not only will the shoes be great, but the service will be as well. Nordstrom is known for going above and beyond in providing personalized service to give all of its patrons an amazing customer experience. You'll probably only be buying one pair of shoes at Nordstrom if you are on a limited budget, but you'll love every minute of the buying experience. After your shopping extravaganza at Nordstrom, you're not likely to offer to treat at the restaurant, but you will certainly look and feel fancy. We thus see that the other dimension of value is quality, which includes the quality of the buying experience.

In making the choice between Payless and Nordstrom, you make the quantity/quality tradeoff and you get what you pay for. Similarly, you need to choose whether your business is going to compete on price or on value. What unique value are you going to offer to the marketplace? Your first decision when starting your business is whether or not you're going to be a Payless or a Nordstrom.

It's usually not a good idea for small businesses to compete on price like Payless does, since they lack the economies of scale that allow large companies to spread overhead across large production and sales bases. While the internet has leveled the playing field a bit in recent years and made it theoretically possible for a small company to sell globally with no more overhead than a website, just because something is possible does not make it smart business strategy. Unless you have access to superior technology or a low-cost, global supply-chain connection, you are probably better off going the value route. As a small company, your overhead can easily be kept down when you make wise spending decisions, so it's better to keep it low and your value high. Be a Nordstrom by looking for ways to

> ### Chic Tip
>
> ASSESS YOUR COMPETITORS' BUSINESS TACTICS AND STYLES. LOOK FOR WAYS THAT YOU CAN CONTRAST THEM. IF THEY DO EVERYTHING IN PERSON, THINK ABOUT TAKING YOUR BUSINESS ENTIRELY ONLINE, OR VICE VERSA. IF THEIR WEBSITES HAVE PICTURES OF COMPUTERS AND BUSINESS PEOPLE, DECORATE YOURS WITH LAUGHING CHILDREN, FRUIT AND VEGETABLES, OR NATURE SCENES.

increase value, such as by providing superior customer service. While your Chic Entrepreneur dream may be grandiose, don't make the mistake of trying to be too much too soon. It is better to start with just the shoe department, and once you create a stronghold, you can expand from there.

⚜ Here are some ways that companies can compete on value:

- Superior quality
- Personalized service
- Knowledge and information
- Speed of delivery
- Ease of use
- Accuracy
- Results
- Vastness of selection
- Specialty products
- Design and aesthetics

Meet Don and Donna

To illustrate this point another way, I'm going to introduce you to Don and Donna, two start-up business owners, and allow you to see for yourself how the decisions they made about their value propositions differ and the resultant effect on the evolution of their businesses.

Don is a plumber who decided to start his own business. He didn't like his boss at his old company and concluded he was just as smart as the owner there, who never seemed to do much real work as far as Don could tell. Don saw how much the company charged for his labor compared to how much he took home and thought about how much money he could make if he were in business for himself. Heck, he could even charge twenty percent less and he'd still be making more. He decided he would give it a try and set up his business. *How hard could it be?* he thought. *It's all just common sense, right?*

He named the company D. H. Plumbing and printed some business cards up at home, put an ad in the Yellow Pages claiming, "Best Prices in Town, No Job Too Small," and was off and running, or so he thought.

Don didn't tell his friends about his business right away; he thought it would be better to tell them in a few months, when he was more successful. His wife told only her closest friends. So, when his wife's best friend asked Don to come over and fix a leaky sink, he gladly took the job. While Don was working, she asked him why he wasn't wearing a D. H. Plumbing uniform and why his company name wasn't on his van. *Jeez, who notices little things like that? I fixed the sink and all she noticed is my clothes. Women,* he thought as he left.

> ### Chic Tip
>
> LOOK FOR WAYS TO INCREASE YOUR WORTH BY ASKING YOUR CUSTOMERS, "HOW CAN WE PROVIDE YOU WITH MORE VALUE?" ASK THEM IF THIS IS SOMETHING THEY WOULD BE WILLING TO PAY MORE TO GET, OR SOMETHING THAT WOULD CAUSE THEM TO DO BUSINESS WITH YOU MORE FREQUENTLY. CREATE PACKAGES THAT OFFER GREATER VALUE, FOR WHICH YOU CAN CHARGE MORE.

As Don pulled into his driveway that night, he was careful to roll up his window when he saw his next-door neighbor Bill out watering his lawn. Don was sure that if he told Bill, a business consultant, about his new venture, Bill would try to tell him a bunch of stuff he already knew. Don didn't want to get into that conversation. *Better to just show him how smart I am by just making it happen,* Don thought.

Business started slowly, but Don had some savings put away that he used to get through the lean times, and gradually the phone started to ring. Don used his cell phone as his business phone so he could answer every call and also keep his costs low—he figured there was no reason to waste money on another phone line. When Don got a call, he typically had to answer the same four questions that everyone asked about price, services, availability, and minimum charge. He never contemplated instituting a process or leveraging technology to eliminate the need to do the same non-value-add task repeatedly; Don was too busy working to contemplate this. However, he did notice some trends and decided to make some adjustments along the way.

When he started out, Don had no minimum charge but found he wasted a lot of time going to people's houses only to discover they were just price shopping. He learned his competitors were charging a seventy-five dollar minimum, so he decided to charge a fifty-dollar minimum to make his services more attractive. With the minimum charge, most people decided to have him go ahead and do the work, and sometimes after he had finished one thing, they would ask him to do something else since he was already there. He needed the money so he was happy to take whatever work he could get, even if it meant going outside his core expertise or rescheduling—and angering—other customers; Don figured they'd get over it because he was the cheapest in town.

Don owned a plain white van and considered painting his company name on the side, but then had second thoughts. That seemed so permanent, and since he was not completely sure yet if this business was really going to work, he decided to play it conservative. *Maybe some dream job with good steady pay will come along,* he would think from time to time after a particularly tough day. He'd heard that most small businesses fail in the first few years and knew a lot of other plumbers who had tried to do their own thing, but ended up deciding to go back to work for someone else. Don wanted his business to work, but he felt like it wasn't really in his control, so he opted for a magnetic sign for the van to keep his

5

options open. *I'll just have to wait and see what happens,* he thought.

Occasionally, a little disquieting voice in his head asked, *What if I fail?* He would try to dismiss it, but the nagging worry lingered and made him further resolve to save money by doing everything himself. Don did all of his own bookkeeping, even though his sister told him that he should hire someone else. When his daughter suggested that he get a website, Don replied, "The plumbing business is all about Yellow Pages advertising, always has been, always will be; everyone knows that."

In fact, his ad did keep the phone ringing, and Don kept busy with all there was to do. So he felt like he was doing well, but at the end of the month he wondered why he was always struggling to pay the bills. He kept hoping that things would change. *It just takes time to establish yourself, right?* he wondered.

Don worked long hours before his sister started chipping in to do the bookkeeping—for free, of course. Why would you pay a family member a salary, especially if there is not a lot of money in the business? Don's brother-in law, Jim, was also a plumber and hit Don up for a job after being fired for coming in late too often. Don really didn't have enough work for him, but hired Jim anyway. Don wasn't sure if he did this because he felt like he had to help out family, or because he didn't want to admit to his brother-in-law that the business wasn't doing so well. Don gave Jim a low-responsibility job where he couldn't screw anything up and thought, *Well at least the business is growing. Now we are a three- person company. Things will surely pick up now. We're doing all the same things as the other guys.*

The next day, Don got a flyer in the mail advertising a small business tips seminar, featuring a business coach and business consultant. *Who has time for stuff like that? I have to run my business,* he thought as he crumpled up the flyer.

In an attempt to give his brother-in-law more to do, Don turned over the cell phone to him. *He can answer all these annoying calls,* Don thought. He was starting to get irritated with having to answer the phone constantly; it was such a distraction when he was on a job, and he felt like he could never get away—even on his lunch break, he was chained to the business. Trying to drum up new business, Don called the Yellow Pages and upgraded his ad to a half page. *This has got to work. I'm running out of money,* he thought. *Pretty soon, I'm going to have to start buying my shoes at Payless.*

Now meet Donna. Donna is a mechanic. She worked on cars growing up, being the only girl in a family with five brothers. She was working as a secretary at a local manufacturing plant, but found her work unfulfilling and began dreaming of doing something that had more meaning to her. After some soul searching, she decided that cars were her true love, and she was willing to take a pay cut to get back to doing something she really enjoyed.

Having brought several cars from disrepair back to life, including the first two she ever owned, she believed in taking care of cars by using preventive maintenance to elongate their usable lives. Donna loved explaining cars to people who didn't have the depth of knowledge she did about them. After talking to a few local shops, she realized that most mechanics didn't really emphasize that aspect, so rather than trying to fit into their mold, she

> ## Chic Tip
>
> SHOP THE COMPETITION. EVERYONE WITHIN YOUR COMPANY NEEDS TO EXPERIENCE THE COMPETITION IN SOME WAY ON AT LEAST AN ANNUAL BASIS. THE BEST WAY TO BECOME MORE COMPETITIVELY INTELLIGENT IN YOUR MARKETPLACE IS TO TEST THE CUSTOMER'S OTHER CHOICES. IF YOUR COMPETITORS KNOW YOU, ASK A FRIEND OR CONSULTANT TO SHOP THE COMPETITION FOR YOU AND REPORT BACK ON THEIR EXPERIENCE.

decided to start her own business.

Before she took the leap, though, Donna recognized that she didn't know what she didn't know and decided to enroll in an evening class on entrepreneurship; she was open to learning from others, rather than letting her ego get in the way. As part of the class, Donna created financial projections for her business and learned how her business model needed to work in order to scale and be profitable. She learned a lot about marketing, specifically about how people buy for psychological reasons, not just practical ones like price, and the importance of choosing a target market and really focusing on giving customers what they want. She also learned about finding a hole in the market where customers' needs were not being adequately met and differentiating her business from the competition by filling that hole. That was when Donna decided to use the uniqueness of being a female mechanic to her advantage. She realized that there was a hole in the market when it came to servicing women's cars. Most car places marketed to men, but women owned just as many cars as men did. Even if they didn't always have as much enthusiasm or knowledge about cars as men did, women still made buying decisions when it came to servicing them.

With her target demographic firmly set, Donna decided to tailor everything she did in her company to the female car owner. She knew she was only going after fifty percent of the market, but she figured she would rather do that well than try to appeal to everyone, and thus generically resonate with no one. Donna knew she would be best at appealing and catering to women, so she chose to focus on her strengths and do what she could do best. After brainstorming and asking her family and friends for their opinions, Donna named her business Ms. Mechanic.

To make it official, Donna spoke with an attorney who set up her company as an LLC and filed the requisite papers with the state. In order to fund her business, Donna presented her business plan to her community bank and convinced it to give her a line of credit. She had to secure the line with her mortgage, but because she knew she was one hundred percent committed to making this work, that didn't seem like a huge risk to her. She knew she had thought through her plan and she believed in herself.

Before picking the location for the business, Donna consulted some female friends, specifically her more upscale girlfriends, who had nice cars that they always kept in tiptop shape. Rather than get opinions from everyone, Donna just wanted to hear what her target demographic thought. She got some good input, and her friends and acquaintances were happy to help by offering advice and support. One woman told Donna that her husband's friend was in commercial retail leasing and later introduced Donna to him. Instead of getting a shop on Highway One, beside all the other mechanics in town, Donna found an affordable location between a day-care center and a grocery store. She figured this would be convenient to her target demographic.

> ## Chic Tip
>
> CULTIVATE YOUR OWN UNIQUE STYLE. TRY CONSISTENTLY WEARING ONE SIGNATURE ITEM LIKE A SCARF OR A PIN OR A SPECIFIC COLOR, OR HAVING A CATCH PHRASE THAT YOU ALWAYS SAY. THIS WILL MAKE YOU BOTH MEMORABLE AND DISTINCTIVE. THINK ANNA WINTOUR AND HER OVERSIZED SUNGLASSES.

Another friend volunteered her daughter, Jenny, who was home from college for the summer, to do some part-time receptionist work for Donna. Donna and her friend convinced Jenny, a sophomore business major, that an "entrepreneurial internship" would look good on her résumé—certainly much better than a job at the corndog stand in the mall. Jenny signed on for minimum wage, excited to watch a startup in action.

To begin her marketing campaign directed toward women, Donna special ordered mechanic suits in pale pink. She had a graphic designer friend design a logo of the silhouette of a woman peering under the hood of a sleek red sports car. Instead of the typical mechanic shop with car magazines everywhere, Donna bought women's magazines and used décor that appealed to women, including cushioned, clean chairs and pastel yellow wallpaper. She also decided that she and future employees would have a commitment to explaining, in detail, everything that was done to the customer's car in layman's terms. Donna also resolved that at Ms. Mechanic, they would provide information to their customers about proactively caring for their cars for safety, performance, and extended life. This was all part of the unique value they would offer to the marketplace.

The Yellow Pages sales rep that Don used came by to try to get Donna to buy an ad, but she decided to invest her money in other things. She leased a billboard that had her business name above the tagline, "Women Under the Hood—Experience the Difference of a Female Mechanic," with a picture of her new logo. Using the billboard for three months cost less than a quarter-page ad in the Yellow Pages for a year. While it was risky to make such a bold move, it ended up getting the attention of some people in the media. A reporter interviewed Donna for a short article that ran alongside a picture of the sign in the local newspaper. Soon after, the story about Donna's shop was picked up by a local radio station and the nightly TV news did a spot about it, as well.

By taking the risk of alienating people not in her target market, Donna made an instant connection with her ideal customers. By daring to be different, she established her niche. Her approach of long-term, proactive care allowed her to encourage her customers to make their appointments in advance and to schedule their regular maintenance checks. Thus, her calendar filled up well in advance and her cash flow became more predictable. After doing competitive research, Donna also decided to charge about fifteen percent more than her nearby competitors did, because she knew that she offered a total experience and her customers were willing to pay for it.

Having someone else answer the phone gave the shop a more professional image from the beginning, made operations more organized, and allowed Donna to spend more time doing the two things she did best: diagnosing cars and nurturing her customer relationships. Her customers appreciated her personal touch and always commented on the cute pink suits with the logo on them. One by one, they told their girlfriends and Donna's clientele started to grow.

Donna had built her business the right way and consequently loved it, instead of starting to resent it as some business owners do. Donna bubbled over with passion and enthusiasm about her business everywhere she went. Instead of complaining or giving a wishy-washy "We'll see how it goes," she was positive and optimistic whenever someone asked about her business and enjoyed telling people about the great things her customers were saying and her plans for growth.

> ### Chic Tip
>
> TAKE A PERSONALITY TEST AND FIND OUT WHAT YOU'RE REALLY GOOD AT. ONCE YOU DETERMINE YOUR STRENGTHS, YOU ARE IN A BETTER POSITION TO BUILD YOUR COMPANY'S UNIQUE VALUE PROPOSITION AROUND THEM. DON'T JUST STRIVE TO BE DIFFERENT—STRIVE TO BE UNIQUELY YOU. THE MORE TIME YOU SPEND DOING WHAT YOU'RE BEST AT, THE MORE VALUE YOU CAN ADD TO THE MARKETPLACE.

Good job candidates started to show up at her door before Donna ever posted an open position. Instead of turning them away, Donna selectively interviewed some of them, assessed her business's needs, and picked up some excellent hires. She didn't want to rely purely on a gut feeling, so Donna put each candidate through a formal interview process and quick personality test, knowing that the person must not only be competent, but also fit within the company culture, have strengths that would match the job responsibilities, and be inspired by the mission of excellent service.

Rather than stick rigidly to the idea of being an all-female mechanic shop, she was flexible with her vision. When she realized how difficult it would be to limit herself to hiring only qualified female mechanics, Donna decided to bring on two male mechanics who were both "A" players and embraced the values of the company. They were smarter than Donna in different areas of the business, and she was happy to have their wisdom on her side. She gave them job descriptions and specific duties and tied their compensation to a bonus based on revenue. Her employees started to tell all of their friends to come to Donna's shop as well. With the new employees, Donna's sales doubled each month for three months straight and continued to grow. Donna used her business plan and her financials to convince her bank to give her a bigger line of credit so she could continue to grow smart.

After a year, Donna opened a second shop and replicated her success. She achieved some economies of scale from her creative marketing efforts that the whole town had started to notice, but she didn't extend herself too far too fast. With the second shop showing a profit in the first month, Donna was also able to upgrade her wardrobe with a few pairs of shoes from Nordstrom.

Don vs. Donna

So what did Don do wrong and Donna do right? We can identify some very important "smart business strategies" and some very common "small business mistakes" in these simplistic stories.

Don entered his business without a plan or any business knowledge and made no attempt to seek it out. Don asked how hard it could be and then proceeded to find out. He started off weak, because he never looked for ways to add unique value. His only motivation for getting into the business was money, so his passion level was low. He failed to start with his friends, family, and neighbors first and advertised the same way that "everyone else" in his industry did. He tried to compete on price and went after any job he could get, instead of getting ideal jobs. Don did not seek outside advice. He failed to see that people were buying not just the result, but also the entire experience with his company. He chose quick cash flow over building long-term trusted relationships and positive good will. He did not commit one hundred percent to making it happen, nor did he take full responsibility for being in charge of the destiny of his business; instead, he just watched what happened. Don hired someone he already knew was a B (probably C) player, because of family and pride, and gave him duties that he had to have known were unsuited for him. He continued to use the same strategy and expected better results.

Donna, on the other hand, came in with a purpose larger than profits and a well-thought-out strategy. She realized that she didn't know it all and pursued outside learning. She conducted her own market research and sought the advice of trusted successful businesspeople. She decided to do something different and emphasized that in her marketing strategy instead of trying to fit in with the rest of her industry. She identified a target market and designed her service with them in mind. She did not compete on price, but instead emphasized her value and quality, turning her service into a complete experience that commanded higher margins.

Donna was passionate and fully committed to the growth of her business. She enlisted the help of her whole network. Realizing that she couldn't do it all herself, she took a team approach from the start and used her own strengths to bring out the best in others and get their assistance by making them see her dream and allowing them to achieve something worthwhile for themselves in the process.

By being bold, she created a PR frenzy and picked up tons of free exposure instead of sinking her advertising dollars into traditional channels. She anticipated her growth needs, created jobs that would increase profits for the company and cover the costs of the people doing them, and hired good people through proper and logical screening and interviewing. Then, she gave her employees clear job descriptions with expectations and an incentive component to make them feel vested in the success of the business.

So What's the Difference?

Why did Don and Donna create such different businesses for themselves? Was it because Don was stupid, unmotivated, or not as creative? Did Donna just get lucky? Make no mistake about it: Don and Donna created their situations, just as we all do every day. Our lives are not created for us. You are the Cinderella picking out your shoe, so if it doesn't fit, there is only one person to blame. And if it does fit, you do deserve the credit. You always deserve the credit, for everything you do, be it good or bad. Successful people take full responsibility for their lives. Step number one toward that success is realizing you are in control. How you manage and think about your business and the types of decisions that you make will determine exactly what kind of business you end up with, flourishing or floundering.

Creating a business is about creating value for others. You will achieve success in the exact proportion to the amount of value you are able to create for the marketplace. Whether your company is a Payless or a Nordstrom, the value proposition that you are providing is the central element of your business model. Everything else builds upon that core, so make sure that your value is solid, genuine, worthwhile, and different.

How Chic are You?

🔺 Do you have a professional headshot? Find a friend who is a good photographer, put on a suit, and stand in front of a neutral background. Take several shots and pick the best one. By preparing for your success, you won't be left scrambling when someone wants to put your picture somewhere and will resist the urge to crop yourself out of a group photo in a pinch.

🔺 Do you have a 100–150 word bio for you and your business?

🔺 Do you have something free you can offer people as a way to sample your experience? If your product is pricey, find a way to eliminate the risk for first- time buyers. A guarantee can serve as both buyers' insurance as well as an internal quality-control standard.

🔺 When you see people you have met before, do they remember you and what you do? If not, you may need to be bolder with your approach. Use an analogy or story to convey what you do to make your value proposition more memorable.

🔺 When people ask you what you do, do you start to sweat, get excited about telling them, or bore them to tears? You'll be asked this question hundreds of times, so invest the thought and effort into making sure you nail

THE ANSWER EVERY TIME. BE ABLE TO EXPLAIN YOUR VALUE IN A FIFTEEN-SECOND ELEVATOR PITCH THAT SOUNDS NATURAL BUT IS PERFECTLY CRAFTED. GIVE PEOPLE JUST ENOUGH INFORMATION TO MAKE THEM WANT MORE.

ARE YOU TRYING TO BE SOMEONE YOU ARE NOT? HAVING INTEGRITY MEANS BEING TRUE TO YOU AND ACTING IN A WAY THAT IS CONSISTENT WITH YOUR INTERNAL FRAMEWORK OF PRINCIPLES. TO PROVIDE TRUE VALUE, YOUR ACTIONS NEED TO BE IN ACCORDANCE WITH YOUR VALUES.

DO YOU HAVE A GOOD ANSWER TO THE QUESTION, "HOW ARE YOU DIFFERENT?" I'VE SEEN BUSINESS OWNERS BECOME THEIR OWN WORST ENEMY IN THE FACE OF THIS QUESTION, SO BE CAREFUL AND STRATEGIC HERE. REALIZE THIS QUESTION IS NOT AN INVITATION TO BASH YOUR COMPETITION; IT IS AN OPPORTUNITY TO DISPLAY YOUR COMPREHENSIVE KNOWLEDGE OF THE MARKETPLACE YOU ARE PLAYING IN. SO MAKE SURE YOU KNOW YOUR TOP COMPETITORS' STRENGTHS AND WEAKNESSES WELL ENOUGH TO NAVIGATE THIS POTENTIAL MINE FIELD WITHOUT BLOWING YOURSELF UP.

OUT OF EVERY TEN PEOPLE YOU TELL WHAT YOU DO, HOW MANY REALLY GET IT? HOW MANY REALLY GET EXCITED ABOUT IT? VALUE IS IN THE EYES OF THE BEHOLDER. WHAT YOU HAVE TO OFFER IS ONLY WORTH ANYTHING IF IT IS WORTH SOMETHING TO THOSE TO WHOM YOU ARE OFFERING IT.

CHAPTER TWO

Wal-Mart or Whole Foods: Pick Your Niche

If you want to buy milk, underwear, a car battery, and some Vicks VapoRub all in one fell swoop, Wal-Mart's the place to go. If, however, you are cooking that extra special Valentine's Day dinner for your vegan boyfriend Chip to make him love you forever, you'd better skip any store with *mart* in the name and head to Whole Foods to buy ingredients for an all-organic feast to show him that you care.

As discussed in Chapter One, unless you have the economies of scale of a Wal-Mart, it will be better for your business to focus on selling to one type of customer well. You want to build a scalable business that provides you, the owner, with the maximum amount of leverage possible. To accomplish this, you must choose a niche to focus on and resist the urge to stray. Stick to your niche and become the absolute best at what you have to offer. Why go far and wide when you can go narrow and deep? Once you gain an initial stronghold in that one area, you can start to expand beyond your niche.

Wal-Mart Stores and Whole Foods Market have both achieved great success using very different strategies. While they both fall under the broad header of grocery stores[1], the similarities end there. Wal-Mart is your classic generalist, your one-stop shop for everything. However, by choosing to target the masses with their massive selection, they made an important strategic business decision. They may sell to a great many people, but they don't sell to everyone. Neither does Whole Foods. In fact, I would venture to guess that there is not a lot of overlap in the customer bases of these two. They sell to totally different niches. In addition to inventory, location choice also affects who their customers are. Most Wal-Marts are located in small towns and rural areas where the cost of living is significantly lower than the urban locations that Whole Foods tends to choose.

Their different strategies and their corporate values are reflected in their different business decisions. The senior citizen greeters at Wal-Mart send a different message than the granola hippies bagging your groceries at Whole Foods. While Whole Foods prides itself on being socially responsible, Wal-Mart has been criticized for shortcomings in this area and is now furiously making amends. Whole Foods is focused on fresh, natural, earth-friendly items for the long-term health of its customers and the planet. Wal-Mart is focused on selling everything it can at the lowest prices possible. What are you focused on?

As a small business, you can't tackle the world all at once. If you try to do too many things right from the get-go, you risk burning out of energy and through your cash before you start seeing significant results. Start with a small niche that is manageable for you and grow out from there. Your original niche should be a narrow one. By concentrating, you'll be sure that your efforts will really shine.

In addition to marketing reasons, there are operational

---

[1] Wal-Mart is the largest grocery retailer in the United States.

business justifications for starting with a tight focus. When you begin with too big of a niche, you end up spreading yourself too thin, and this is one of those rare cases where being too thin is not a good thing. When you try to do too much, less value is realized from your efforts. However, if you are able to perform at your maximum productivity level, you will put yourself in a position to build the necessary scale into your business. You can then develop a full line of products and services for every niche you can find, because they will be built upon the foundation of your first solid victory. At this point, it becomes a game of cross-sells and up-sells. By claiming a small and well-defined niche, you can dominate a small and well-defined market.

The Chic Entrepreneur realizes it is easier to get well known one market at a time, just as it is to get into one social circle at a time. Once you are well known in one market, you can scale your business by expanding into other areas, but this only works if you have first achieved success on a small scale. This way, every successive product or service you roll out will become more and more profitable. You will need less advertising and less convincing as you expand, because you are building on an already-solid reputation. Picking the right initial niche is the key that will unlock the rest of your entrepreneurial kingdom.

> ### Chic Tip
>
> READ AND WRITE. READ ONE NEW BUSINESS BOOK EVERY MONTH. ONCE YOU ACCOMPLISH THIS, INCREASE IT TO EVERY WEEK. WHILE YOU READ, KEEP A NOTEPAD NEXT TO YOU SO THAT YOU CAN JOT DOWN HOW WHAT YOU ARE LEARNING APPLIES TO YOUR BUSINESS AND YOUR THOUGHTS FOR HOW TO IMPLEMENT THOSE IDEAS IN YOUR COMPANY.

Think of a premium niche as box seats at a football game, and the entire stadium crowd as other business owners in the marketplace. Everyone is getting to watch and experience the same game. However, some people are in the nosebleed section with binoculars, buying Bud Light and peanuts from a grimy, smelly stand (and paying ridiculous prices for them), while others are in the boxes, sipping champagne, being waited on by cute waiters in tuxedos, mingling with other successful people, and getting a great view of all the action. So which seats would you rather have? This is the power of focus.

Now it's time for you to do some work. To help you narrow your focus and pick your perfect niche, write out a description of your ideal clients. Don't worry; I've done most of the work for you. All you have to do is fill in the blanks below. If you think of other important details to add, you can tack them on at the end.

My ideal clients are (male / female) between the ages of
_____ and _____. They live in the _____ area(s) of
_____ city(ies) in _____ state(s). They live in a
(house / condo / apartment). They are (married / single /
divorced). They (do / do not) have children. They pay with
(cash / credit / check) (on time / early / late). They purchase
from us (daily / weekly / monthly / yearly / once in a lifetime).
They contact us (frequently / rarely / never). They require (a
lot / very little) hand holding through the sales and/or
service process. Their budget for our product is $_____.
They see our product / service as (valuable / incidental). They
are (white / blue) collar. They are (wealthy / middle-class /
poor). They make $_____ a year, and work about
_____ hours a week. Their hobbies are _____,
_____, and _____. Their values

are _____, _____, and _____. When it comes to our product / service, they are really not all that concerned about _____, but _____ is really important. They are willing to pay more in order to get _____. They would be happy to live without _____, in exchange for a discount. What makes my clients different from others in this market is that they always _____, they never _____, they love to _____, and they hate to _____. My clients always remember _____, but they frequently forget _____.

Some other important things to remember about my clients are:

_____

_____

_____

Obviously, your customers may fall into more than one of the above categories, and some of these may not apply to them. However, the point is for you to narrow your focus until you create a very clear picture of exactly the type of client you want to do business with. You want to be able to describe them succinctly to others by saying, "My best clients are…" or "My ideal clients are…"

or "My favorite clients are..." or "The people who seem to get the best value from us/enjoy our services the most/rave about us to all of their friends are..." or "What our customers like best about us is that we...."

The more you can make statements like this to others, the more your vision of your ideal clients will come alive in their minds as well as yours. It is with that kind of clear focus that your business really starts to take shape. Before you have a strategy, your business idea is just like a dress hanging on a hanger. Formulating your strategy puts it on a mannequin. Now, you can see what it will look like when you put it on.

Many business owners, like Don from Chapter One, make the mistake of selling to anyone and everyone and will take whatever revenue they can get. They think that since they need the business, trying to get it from anywhere is the best way to get more.

Picking a niche is counterintuitive because you are consciously deciding to sell to fewer people. You are narrowing the pool of people you are willing to sell to, but by doing so, you are increasing your attractiveness to your target market by declaring that you want to work only with them. Everyone prefers to buy from someone who specializes in people like them. When you narrow your focus, you will find that you'll be able to sell more total goods and services at a higher profit. You will also become better known faster by concentrating on one area and thus generate more word-of-mouth.

Chic Caution

DON'T GET SO CAUGHT UP IN THE DAY-TO-DAY WORK THAT YOU LOSE SIGHT OF THE BIG PICTURE OF WHAT YOU ARE TRYING TO ACCOMPLISH. DEVELOP A VISION FOR YOUR BUSINESS. WRITE A MISSION STATEMENT THAT INCLUDES WHAT YOU PROVIDE TO WHOM AND HOW AND WHAT IMPACT YOU WANT TO MAKE. KEEP IT SUCCINCT BUT MAKE IT COMPLETE. IT CAN BE THREE TO FIVE SENTENCES IN LENGTH, AND YOU SHOULD BE ABLE TO SUM IT UP IN SEVEN WORDS OR LESS.

If you are selling a Ferrari and you market it to everyone, you'll waste ninety-nine percent of your marketing efforts. If you sell that same Ferrari to men in their forties and fifties, who wear Armani suits, dine at five-star restaurants, and frequently travel abroad, you will be much more effective. First, your message will speak directly to their specific needs, wants, and desires. Second, you already have done some initial qualification based on easy demographic factors that make them more likely to be in the market for what you have to sell. Finally, once you have narrowed down exactly who you are looking for, you will be able to find and get your message before them more easily. Just like selling a Ferrari, there are certain types of people who are in the market for exactly what you have to sell and are willing to pay for it, and there are others who are not. Don't worry about the others; focus on your niche.

The Chic Entrepreneur knows that there are riches in niches, so her strategy is to build her business empire one niche at a time. How does a Chic Entrepreneur pick her niche? She infuses her personality, her past, her passion, her purpose, and her intuition into her focused business strategy. Let's take a closer look at these characteristics:

Personality: Personalities, by their very nature, are different. The Chic Entrepreneur revels in her authenticity. She is true to herself, her style, and her values. She creates a business that fits her and the life she wishes to live.

Past: Everything that has happened to her gives her increased knowledge and strength to go forward. She realizes that challenges are merely learning experiences, and failure and defeat are necessary parts of success.

Passion: The Chic Entrepreneur is full of energy and enthusiasm. She believes in herself and in her business. Her

diplomacy wise

23 ⬩

confidence is not arrogance, but rather an ease with who she is and the value she has to offer.

Purpose: The Chic Entrepreneur has a purpose beyond profits and larger than a P&L statement. She strives to make a difference in people's lives by using her talents for the larger good of humanity.

Intuition: The Chic Entrepreneur uses her instincts. She realizes that only she can have access to her instincts, so only she can use them. This can be a big differentiator and competitive advantage, so don't let the fear of sounding "too out there" scare you away from using one of your secret *woman* weapons.

Meet Rhonda and Rodica

Let's examine how having a focused strategy actually plays out by taking a look at two more entrepreneurs, Rhonda and Rodica.

Rhonda has her own event planning company, Events 'R' Us. She started her company with a friend and they have been in business for four years. During that time, the two partners have done corporate event planning, weddings, retirement parties, birthday parties, bar mitzvahs, funerals, and any other events that have come their way.

Rhonda has never turned down a job, no matter how small. Lately, though, she has been doing the weddings of many of her friends who tend to demand a lot of her time and then expect the "friend discount." Rhonda wishes that she could break into a wealthier clientele base, but for now, she takes any job that she can get. While she enjoys doing weddings the most, she finds that she makes more money from big corporate events. The latter are harder to come by, however, and she figures she'd be crazy to turn down any work at this point.

Rhonda has difficulty competing for corporate events against firms that work exclusively for corporations and have extensive portfolios. She hopes that in a few years she'll have a larger portfolio of corporate work to show. In the meantime, Rhonda's niche can be summed up as any gathering of any people for any purpose. How narrow is that? Despite being happy to take whatever she could get, Rhonda wasn't getting much. In an effort to raise her margins, she decided to stop buying her party supplies at Party City and instead headed over to Super Wal-Mart to see what she could find and do some grocery shopping. With such a lack of focus, let's hope she can find her way out.

> **Chic Tip**
>
> CREATE A BOARD OF ADVISORS. YOUR BOARD SHOULD CONSIST OF FIVE TO SEVEN PEOPLE WITH VARIED EXPERTISE. INCLUDE AN ATTORNEY, AN ACCOUNTANT, A MARKETING PERSON, SOMEONE WITH GOOD KNOWLEDGE OF THE MARKETPLACE YOU ARE IN, AND SOMEONE WHO HAS STARTED OR RUN A BUSINESS BEFORE. HAVE A BOARD MEETING AT LEAST TWICE A YEAR TO GET THEIR INPUT. HAVE AN AGENDA. GIVE AN UPDATE OF KEY METRICS, CHALLENGES, GOALS, AND TACTICS THAT YOU ARE PLANNING TO EXECUTE, AND THEN OPEN DISCUSSION. BE RECEPTIVE TO THEIR FEEDBACK AND MAKE SURE THEY KNOW YOU APPRECIATE THEIR TIME.

Now meet Rodica. Rodica is an interior decorator. Just before she started her business, she helped her parents move from the five-bedroom suburban house she'd grown up in to a two-bedroom apartment in the city. As they went from room to room and through box after box, making difficult decision about what to keep and what to toss, it occurred to Rodica that downsizing is a big problem that many baby boomers would be facing in the near future. She enjoyed this work. Her diplomacy and sensitivity, combined with her ability to help others make wise decisions, made her good at it. She decided this would be her niche: working exclusively with people who were downsizing and helping them through this transition and all of its decorating implications.

A few months after she dove into the business, a family moved into a house in her neighborhood and heard through the grapevine that she was a decorator. They were upgrading from a one-bedroom apartment and needed new furniture and some artwork to fill their new three-bedroom house; they asked Rodica if she would help them. Despite this being a potentially lucrative job, Rodica recognized that these were not her ideal clients and, instead of taking the job for the money, referred them to an interior decorator friend of hers who specialized in suburban homes. That same friend subsequently sent Rodica a couple who was downsizing and moving into the city. When Rodica spoke to them on the phone, she immediately recognized what area of town they were in, right by the new Whole Foods. When they told her that they shopped there all the time because they were both vegetarians, Rodica asked if they would like to look at some of her green designs. They were thrilled with her suggestions. Since she was a specialist, she knew her clients well, before she even met them.

Rhonda vs. Rodica

> **Chic Tip**
>
> WRITE A BUSINESS PLAN. DON'T TRY TO DO IT IN ONE DAY; SPACE IT OUT OVER TIME. SPEND A FEW HOURS A WEEK ON IT FOR ONE MONTH. UNLESS YOU WILL BE PRESENTING IT TO SOMEONE ELSE, DON'T WORRY ABOUT MAKING ALL THE WORDING PERFECT. FIND A TEMPLATE ONLINE AND USE THE OUTLINE FORMAT, RATHER THAN PARAGRAPHS. DOING THIS WILL KEEP YOU FOCUSED AND YOUR PLAN BRIEF.

Rhonda is not growing her business in a chic way. By vying for every event she can find, she comes across as scattered and slightly desperate. Despite casting a wide net, she is not catching very much because she has not positioned herself effectively as being really good at any one thing. Other event planners don't send work her way because she is their competition, and potential clients are wary of her lack of in-depth experience in any one area. Even her friends don't take her business seriously and probably think they are doing her a favor by giving her the opportunity to gain some experience. Rhonda does not have a big enough company to do so many different kinds of events. Furthermore, she makes the mistake of thinking that things will change with time, if she just keeps on keeping on. While persistence is a worthy and effective value, it needs to be combined with continuous learning and refining of strategy. Once you pick a strategy, you need to assess what is working and what is not and make adjustments along the way.

Rodica, on the other hand, has a focused niche. She is not everyone's competition in the interior decorating world; she is carving out her own focused domain. Therefore, she refers clients to others and they, in turn, do the same for her because they know she is an expert. Unlike Rhonda, who must embark on a new learning curve with each client she takes on due to her disparate range of events, Rodica is honing her expertise and learning how to do her job faster, better, and cheaper, while maintaining her standard of high-quality work so her good reputation continues to grow.

Take some time to plot out your own focused strategy. You build off your strengths, so pick a niche

> ### Chic Tip
>
> HOLD A STRATEGY SESSION EVERY SIX MONTHS, THE RESULT OF WHICH SHOULD ULTIMATELY FIT ON AN INDEX CARD. DECEMBER AND JUNE ARE GOOD TIMES UNLESS YOU ARE IN RETAIL, IN WHICH CASE I SUGGEST JANUARY AND JULY. SET GOALS FOR THE NEXT SIX MONTHS, ONE YEAR, AND THREE YEARS. DETERMINE TACTICS FOR HOW YOU PLAN TO ACCOMPLISH THOSE GOALS. THEN EVERY SIX MONTHS, ASSESS HOW YOU DID AND INCORPORATE ANY NEW DEVELOPMENTS INTO THE PLAN. REFRESH YOUR GOALS, MAKING SURE THEY ARE STILL RELEVANT AND THE TIMEFRAMES ARE STILL APPROPRIATE. WRITE YOUR NEW SIX-MONTH GOALS ON ANOTHER INDEX CARD AND TAPE IT TO YOUR DESK FOR DAILY REFERENCE. WHENEVER YOU FEEL YOU ARE LOSING YOUR FOCUS OR HAVE CONFLICTING PRIORITIES, REFERENCE YOUR CARD.

that you are suited for and have a natural advantage in serving. Start by looking for one that other people are either not serving or not sufficiently meeting customers' needs. As an entrepreneur, remember that your business exists to solve people's problems. When clients come to you, they have a specific problem and are seeking a specific solution. When you have a niche, you can show them that you have the exact solution for their particular problem. They will see you as a specialist rather than a generalist and that you specialize in them. When people know that you have exactly what they need, the sales process takes care of itself.

How Chic are You?

🔺 CAN SOMEONE TELL IMMEDIATELY WHAT YOU DO UPON ENTERING YOUR PLACE OF BUSINESS OR YOUR WEBSITE? DON'T MAKE YOUR PASSION A SECRET. MAKE SURE THE ESSENCE OF YOUR BUSINESS COMES THROUGH LOUD AND CLEAR.

🔺 DO YOU USE WORDS THAT YOU DON'T UNDERSTAND AND CAN'T EASILY DEFINE? IF SO, STOP. MISTAKENLY THROWING OUT MADE-UP WORDS LIKE OBLIVIATED AND REPLUDIATING TO TRY TO SOUND SMART WON'T WIN YOU ANY CHIC POINTS. BEING CONFIDENT IN WHO YOU ARE AND WHAT YOU DO KNOW, WILL.

🔺 WOULD ANYONE DISAGREE WITH YOUR APPROACH? IF YOU HAVEN'T DEFIED CONVENTIONAL WISDOM IN ANY WAY, OR DONE ANYTHING THAT WOULD STIR UP A CONTRASTING POINT OF VIEW, YOU MAY BE TOO CONSERVATIVE. A SMALL BUSINESS IS LIKE A SAILBOAT DRIFTING AT SEA. OCCASIONALLY, YOU GET LUCKY AND CATCH A BREEZE, BUT STRATEGICALLY YOU NEED TO MAKE YOUR OWN WAVES OR YOU ARE NOT GOING TO GET ANYWHERE. IN ORDER TO GET KNOWN, YOU NEED TO TAKE A STAND AND DO NEW THINGS.

🔺 WHAT DOES YOUR BUSINESS STAND FOR? OBVIOUSLY YOU ARE IN BUSINESS TO MAKE MONEY, BUT WHAT IS THE LARGER MISSION THAT YOU WISH TO ACCOMPLISH? HOW DO

YOU WANT YOUR BUSINESS TO INFLUENCE THE WORLD AROUND IT? IT IS IMPORTANT TO HAVE A PURPOSE BEYOND PROFITS; KNOWING YOURS WILL BE A GUIDING COMPASS IN TIMES OF DECISION.

ARE YOU CONSIDERED AN EXPERT IN YOUR FIELD? MAKE YOURSELF SLIGHTLY FAMOUS BY BECOMING KNOWN AMONGST YOUR PEERS, GETTING INVOLVED IN ORGANIZATIONS AND SERVING ON COMMITTEES AND IN LEADERSHIP POSITIONS. THE ONLY WAY TO EARN OTHERS' RESPECT IS TO SHOW THEM WHAT YOU CAN DO.

HAVE YOU WRITTEN ANYTHING ON YOUR FIELD OF EXPERTISE? IT DOESN'T TAKE LONG TO AUTHOR AN ARTICLE OR A TOP-TEN TIPS LIST. PEOPLE WHO SAY SMART THINGS MAKE AN IMPRESSION IN THE MOMENT. PEOPLE WHO WRITE SMART THINGS MAKE AN IMPRESSION OVER A LIFETIME. TAKE THE TIME TO PUT A BIT OF YOUR EXPERTISE DOWN ON PAPER TO MAGNIFY ITS POWER AND ITS VALUE.

DOES YOUR MISSION STATEMENT HAVE REAL MEANING OR IS IT JUST A BUNCH OF FLOWERY LANGUAGE? YOU WANT A MISSION THAT IS CRISP, CLEAR, AND MEMORABLE, AND THAT REPRESENTS THE HEART AND SOUL OF THE BUSINESS. THIS WILL UNITE YOUR TEAM WHEN IT IS IMPLEMENTED INTO YOUR OPERATIONAL FRAMEWORK THROUGH THE DAILY ACTIONS, INTENTIONS, AND ATTITUDES OF YOUR EMPLOYEES.

CHAPTER THREE

T.J. Maxx or the Tailor: What Do Customers Really Want?

Imagine you have a big social event coming up and you need a new outfit. Would you rather go somewhere where you know you'll probably end up with something that's not quite the right color, doesn't really match, and doesn't exactly fit, but looks decent, will keep you from being naked, and will get you by for the moment? Or would you rather consult a fashion designer who will take into account all the unique features and benefits of your body and create something perfect for your special night? The first dress might seem like a great deal (as long as you can get out those deodorant stains from the last person who tried it on and the footprint on the sleeve from when someone stepped on it in the fitting room), but in an ideal world, which shopping trip would you rather experience?

I've shopped for clothes off the rack and off the discount rack and know both can yield some great finds. However, slogging through the narrow aisles of T.J. Maxx isn't always an activity I have time for or want to partake in. There is nothing better than going to a skilled tailor, being carefully measured, and coming away with a suit that handsomely and snugly fits your body to a T. Your customers feel the same way. It costs more to create customized solutions, but people will pay more for a tailored fit. Just take a look at any buying situation from the customers' perspective: They don't want what you have; they want exactly what they want. In order to satisfy your customers, you need to have an understanding of not just their needs, but also how they wish to experience what you have, as part of their lives. The goal is to give them a product that fits in with them and is a natural complement to their existing lifestyle, not to convince them to change the way they do things so that they can do business with you. Your customers are a reflection of your business. Just like looking in a mirror, when you focus on the customers, your customers will focus on you. You want active customers who make decisions with delight, not by default.

To determine what your customers want, ask yourself these questions:

- How much time do we spend finding out about our customers before we try to sell them what we have?
- Does our marketing material speak to our customers' specific needs instead of just giving a general overview of our services?
- When it comes to the product/service we sell, if our customers had twice the budget, what would they buy?
- How can we make what we provide feel more one-of-a-kind instead of mass-produced?

Be the Tailored Fit:
Give Your Customers What They Want

Tailoring your products and services to customers' needs in order to give them exactly what they want is not as difficult as it sounds, because the intangible elements of what you are selling are often just as, if not more, important than the tangible elements. Much of what people purchase is wrapped up in the *psychology of buying*— an aspect of sales that many businesses neglect and only a few smart ones embrace. The main reason that people shell out their hard-earned money is to make themselves feel good, whether that be in the form of wanting to feel happy, beautiful, decadent, healthy, loving, or any host of other pleasure-seeking motivations. More commonly than most sellers realize, customers buy for emotional reasons, not just physical ones. I know I do. When was the last time you bought something because you needed an emotional pick-me-up?

In order to satisfy your customers, you need to make their buying experience an emotional one, not than just a handoff. Businesses that embrace their customers' psyche create loyal customers. Who wants many customers who buy from them only once? It may seem like a good short-term plan to get a blip in cash flow, but that is not the way to build a business. As an entrepreneur who is serious about building a company of value, you want many satisfied customers who will buy from you many times. These loyal customers will allow you to turn your entrepreneurial venture into a real business.

What does loyalty mean? Loyalty is defined as having an emotional bond to a brand. Think Starbucks.

> ### Chic Tip
>
> TAKE ONE OF YOUR BEST CUSTOMERS OUT FOR COFFEE ONCE A MONTH AND PICK THAT PERSON'S BRAIN. ASK QUESTIONS LIKE, "WHAT'S YOUR FAVORITE PART OF DOING BUSINESS WITH US?" AND "WHAT'S YOUR LEAST FAVORITE PART?" THE INFORMATION YOU'LL GAIN ON THESE VISITS IS WORTH MORE THAN A WHOLE HILL OF COFFEE BEANS. PLUS, YOU'LL STRENGTHEN THE RELATIONSHIP WITH YOUR CUSTOMER, GET OUT OF THE OFFICE, AND HAVE A BIT OF FUN. ONCE THEY SEE HOW MUCH YOU CARE, YOU MAY EVEN WIND UP WITH A REFERRAL.

↑ Nice questions to ask on the website.

How many people have to have their Starbucks every day, will drive out of their way to get it, and will pay more than a sensible budget would allocate for coffee expenditures? True loyalty is unconditional. It doesn't depend on price or convenience. Once you have demonstrated that you can provide a consistent, positive, and memorable experience, these customers will go out of their way just to buy from you. Loyal customers identify your company with a piece of themselves. They have made your brand a part of their lives. Loyalty is not habit, but a combination between conscious preference and unconscious longing. Loyalty is finding that special place in a customer's heart, where you are their favorite. Loyalty is as close to love as business gets.

So why is your goal to create loyal customers?

1. **Loyal customers keep coming back,** and each time they do, you earn revenue from them. Once they are loyal, you no longer need to coax them to do business with you via a sales pitch or extensive advertising or educate them about what you do; therefore, they are less expensive to acquire. Like a good dog, they just come when called because they like you and they know the routine. Customer loyalty creates reoccurring revenue at increasingly higher margins.

2. **Loyal customers will buy everything you have.** When they like you, they'll want to buy all that you have that suits them. Once you sell someone and deliver something that meets or exceeds their expectations, they will attribute their positive thoughts about that experience to everything that you offer. So the next time they have a need that falls under your product/service umbrella, they will come straight to you. You can cross-sell and up-sell loyal customers more easily and get more of their total business.

3. **Loyal customers are less price-sensitive.** Customers who are loyal tend not to shop around for the lowest price in town. They know that trying somewhere new can be hit or miss. People get into habits and they like routine. They don't mind paying a bit more once they find a company that consistently provides exactly what they want. They prefer to stick with someone they know they can depend on. Price becomes secondary when a customer becomes loyal.

4. **Loyal customers are walking and talking billboards.** Loyal customers provide better advertising than Super Bowl Sunday. Loyal customers say nice things about you to their friends, families, and their entire networks. Such word-of-mouth is priceless, in both senses of the word: It is free and it is the most effective advertising you could ever ask for. If you can create evangelists out of your customers, you can spend half as much on advertising as your closest competition. People trust people. Customers take the recommendations of their friends and families, and even total strangers they perceive to be impartial, as real authority. What comes out of customers' mouths about your business is far more important than what gets written in your advertising copy or on your website.

5. **Loyal customers are actually cheaper to serve.** Once customers are loyal, they tend to complain less and require less of your time to service. They know the system and they trust you; they've been through the learning curve of how you do business, so they service themselves where they can and take up less time. When there is a problem or a mistake, they also complain less and give you the benefit of the doubt more often.

How do you get loyal customers? You give them the emotional experience they crave. As our world has become more wired and wireless, society has become very impersonal. With the increased prevalence of technology like cell phones, PDAs, Bluetooth, and satellite TV, people are starved for a sense of personal connection in our mass-produced world. People long for a good old-fashioned toothy smile, instead of the customary email. From work to play, many of our daily experiences have become dominated by cold, faceless entities. When was the last time you went to a bank and spoke to a teller about your account or pulled up to a gas station to have an attendant run over and pump your gas and wash your windshield? Pressured to reduce costs to offset obscene overhead, many big businesses have sacrificed personal interaction with their customers. That's where you've got the advantage.

As an entrepreneur, you can be the face that your customer has been missing, the voice over the phone instead of a recorded message. Many small businesses worry about the downside of being small, but there is a lot of upside to your size. Most customers are fed up with being treated like a number by giant corporate machines. You can take the customer experience beyond transactional to relational. Make doing business with your company a personal experience. Genuine human interaction is distinctive these days, and you will be remembered for it. Your customers will know that you are not a large business, they will be happy about it, and they will want to form a relationship with your company.

> ## Chic Tip
>
> CREATE A CUSTOMER COMMUNITY. WHETHER IT'S A BLOG OR A REGULAR EVENT OR SOCIAL GATHERING AT YOUR PLACE OF BUSINESS, GIVE YOUR CUSTOMERS A WAY TO MEET EACH OTHER AND LEARN FROM EACH OTHER'S EXPERIENCES. WHEN YOU CAN TIE DOING BUSINESS WITH YOUR COMPANY TO A PART OF THEIR PERSONAL IDENTITY, YOU ARE WELL ON YOUR WAY TO LOYALTY. WHEN YOU CAN TIE IT TO THEIR SOCIAL IDENTITY, YOU ARE THERE.

Think about other ways you can make the experience memorable for the customer. Memorable experiences are driven by our senses. Every sight, sound, smell, taste, and touch will go into forming a memory of your company in the customer's mind, so find a way to maximize their sensual experience. Be eager to solve your customers' problems and passionate about the value that your company provides to them. Remember, this is your life's work, or at least an investment of years of your time. You are building a company of value that will hopefully continue beyond your involvement. This business will be part of your legacy. People will remember not only what you sold, but also how you did it. How can you not be passionate about that?

Creating personal experiences cultivates long-term relationships with customers. Customers who feel like they have a connection with your company will invest in that relationship by giving you feedback on how you are doing and suggestions of other things you could offer. These gems of wisdom can be a continual source of ideas for growth and improvement. Building long-term relationships takes more time, but ultimately those relationships bear more fruit than a one-night stand.

Meet Barbara and Benita

Notice what decisions Barbara and Benita have made regarding their customers and how their choices have affected their businesses.

Barbara is a hairstylist who owns her own salon and rents out chairs to other stylists. After working closely with other small salons for two decades, Barbara figured she knew the business side of running a salon and decided to do it on her own. She bought an old barber shop with her savings, installed four new chairs, put a fresh coat of light blue paint on the walls, placed ads for stylists, and had a sign made with the business name, Cut Loose, in bold print.

Barbara stocked the salon with a variety of magazines and soft drinks, water, and other refreshments to offer the customers, just like in the high-end salons. During her first week in business, Barbara pampered her customers and felt giddy with excitement about owning her own business.

As time rolled on, however, Barbara began forgetting to offer her clients anything to drink or read before starting to work on their hair. When she noticed her overhead creeping up on her monthly financials, she stopped offering drinks altogether and only brought in magazines from home or ones that she received for free. When she first opened, Barbara had allotted one hour per appointment to give her ample time to get to know each customer and find out what style would suit him or her. However, once things got going, she figured she knew most of her customers well enough and they knew what kind of cut they liked, so she reduced appointment times to forty-five minutes to allow her to see more people in a day. Barbara wanted her clients to be happy with her work and tried to offer them what she thought they would like. She kept up on the latest trends in hairstyles, but since she assumed everyone else did, too, she rarely brought up this valuable insight unless someone specifically asked. If a client was unsure of what they wanted,

> ## Chic Tip
>
> PROVIDE CUSTOMERS AN EASY MEANS OF GIVING YOU FEEDBACK. EVERYONE WISHES THEY COULD GET INSIDE THE HEADS OF THEIR CUSTOMERS. FUNNY THING IS MOST CUSTOMERS WOULD LOVE TO GIVE YOU A PIECE OF THEIR MIND, IF YOU ONLY MADE IT CONVENIENT FOR THEM TO DO SO. CUSTOMER EVALUATION FORMS, COMMENT CARDS, SURVEYS, AND FOLLOW-UP CALLS ARE ALL EASY WAYS TO GET FEEDBACK. DON'T HIDE FROM COMPLAINTS; USE THEM TO IDENTIFY AREAS FOR IM- PROVEMENT. PUBLICIZE THE COMPLIMENTS ON A BULLETIN BOARD FOR ALL TO SEE. THE SIGNAGE CAN SAY SOMETHING LIKE, "WE LOVE OUR CUSTOMERS AND OUR CUSTOMERS LOVE US!"

*Give me a piece of your mind

✗ pass

Barbara would drag out her old portfolio of hairstyles. Although many of the pictures were outdated, she figured they could still give clients some good ideas. As soon as someone selected a style, Barbara went straight to work. She didn't ask, "Why do you like that style?" or "Do you realize that you will have to blow dry and curl your hair every day to achieve that same look?" Since she had heard that the customer is always right, she didn't contradict her customers, even when they picked styles that might not flatter them.

After a year in business, Barbara couldn't figure out why she wasn't drawing in more long-term customers. She cut hair well, and as far as she could tell her three associates did, too; however, they all seemed to have a fairly high rate of one-time clients who came in because of their proximity to the salon and were never seen again. Occasionally, one would come back needing a last-minute emergency haircut, but it was obvious Cut Loose was not their first choice.

Barbara began giving her clients discount cards to use and give to their friends. Soon, few people came into the salon without a discount card in hand. It was as if people only came if they got a discount because they knew that discount cards were available. Instead of getting more loyal clients, Barbara devalued her service and thus decreased her revenue.

Barbara stopped giving out discount cards, but she still had many one-time clients and very few regulars. While she was technically in business, it was hardly booming. Barbara had been planning to redecorate her salon with some nice artwork to add to the ambiance, but as she looked over her sales figures for the last quarter, she decided a few prints from the clearance rack at T.J. Maxx would have to do.

Now meet Benita. Benita worked for high-end spas for ten

years saving up and preparing to launch her business. She started her foray into entrepreneurship with what I call a "spare bedroom business," having built a relaxing oasis, equipped with all the amenities right in her spare bedroom. She bought all the waxing, facial, and massage products; set up a heavy-duty, luxurious massage table in the middle of the room; and put in track lighting that she could dim to create just the right mood for relaxation. She painted the walls a calming violet and hung dark plum-colored draperies over the windows. Benita moved her sound system into the room and bought some soothing music and aromatherapy candles, along with aloe plants and parlor palms to increase the beauty in the room and the oxygen in the air.

Benita transformed the adjoining bathroom into a changing room for her customers. There, she installed the same dimmable mood lighting overhead, painted the walls dark mauve, and placed scented candles by the sink, next to refreshing organic mints.

Benita also made sure she had a full stock of teas, waters, and champagne to offer her clients; she knew that relaxation should begin with hydration, especially since it was often neglected during a hectic day. She also knew that many clients got spa treatments because they had something to celebrate, hence the champagne. Benita hoped the setting she created would make her clients forget that they were in a nearby neighborhood and feel like they were at a resort far from their worries and stressors.

To add a personal touch, Benita hung several of her boyfriend Taylor's unframed oil paintings in both the spa and changing rooms. The rich jewel tones in the abstract works meshed with her décor and would encourage her customers' minds to wander at ease.

At first, Benita started her spare bedroom business in her spare time. She told her friends and family what she was doing and slowly started seeing clients. Benita wanted her clients to feel an immediate sense of calm upon entering her spa and therefore made sure the aromatherapy candles were already burning sweet scents into the air when they arrived. Since most of her clients had stressful corporate jobs, Benita wanted the thoughts of their crazy days to melt away like the wax from the glowing wicks. After showing her clients to the changing room and giving them a luxurious blue robe, Benita offered them a warm cup of chamomile tea, water, or champagne and seated them in a plush white recliner. Rather than bombarding them with questions about their day, she would finish paperwork for a few minutes in her bedroom, giving them time to enjoy their beverage and unwind. She knew it was important for her customers to feel completely unhurried and relaxed; even those first few minutes were part of the total experience she was creating for them. When she came back into the spa room, Benita would ask her customers what they would like her to work on. If they wanted a massage, she asked if they had any aches, pains, or other problem areas she could focus on. After assessing the customer's specific needs, Benita got to work. Her clients often told her that they thought they were in heaven.

Benita's business continued to grow as she continued to delight her customers. Benita found that she had far more loyal regulars than one-time customers. After a year, she rented space for her services and commissioned Taylor to paint a beautiful and eye-catching sign for the business, which she aptly named Heaven on Earth.

How Do These Examples Apply to You?

There are business owners like Barbara everywhere you go. They have good intentions and a decent business model, but when it comes to creating a customer experience, they are content to meet expectations and make no effort to exceed them. They aim for adequate, not exceptional, and it shows. There are many little things they could do to endear themselves to their customers and specialized expertise and advice they could provide that would make them a valuable and even indispensable resource, but they don't. Perhaps because the failure to make that extra effort is not a line item on their financials, it doesn't seem important, but it will definitely show in the bottom line. Barbara's service was okay, but when was the last time you heard someone rave about an "OK haircut"?

To earn customer loyalty, you want to run your business like Benita. You want to focus on every detail of your customer's experience, from the moment they walk in to two months after they purchase. That is the time span through which you can give them the pleasantries, the amenities, and the follow-up courtesies that will keep them coming back for more. No matter what you are selling, the customer always has a choice of buying from you, getting something similar somewhere else, or going without. You need to make the first option the clear favorite choice. What will make them loyal is the experience.

Also, be careful not to discount your products and services or devalue them by running perpetual sales or special promotions like Barbara. That only begs the question, "Could I get it cheaper again?" Women tend to have issues with demanding a fair price for their products and services. As a gender, we are pleasers and are inclined to be uncomfortable talking about money, so we discount and devalue our products and services to make people happy and to get that part of the discussion over with. When someone asks, "So how much?" this is often enough to make our eye contact get shifty, our palms start to sweat, and the room suddenly heat up. In this self-created sauna, we start to bargain with ourselves and proceed to negotiate the price of our services lower and lower until we've about given away the farm, just so that we don't hurt the feelings of the person we are talking to. We skip on out of there, thrilled that we got the deal, but that skip soon turns into a kick in our own behind when we realize what a raw deal we gave ourselves. I know it has taken me a lot of practice and conditioning to get to the point where I can talk calmly and confidently about the price of what my company sells.

There is no reason to feel uncomfortable talking about money. A Chic Entrepreneur can talk about money and power as easily as she can talk about the weather, for talking about the forces of business is just as natural as talking about the sun and the rain. Money and power exist out in the open for us all to see and experience. A Chic Entrepreneur makes no qualms about desiring them, nor does she succumb to outdated gender stereotypes that say it is unfeminine to do so. She realizes that business revolves around money; as a businesswoman, there is no hiding from it. It is everywhere. A business owner who is scared to talk money is like a swimmer who is scared to talk about the water. So, psych yourself up with an "I'm worth it" mantra and dive into those money conversations with confidence. Of course, men often have similar trepidations; however, since women have trouble earning as much as their male equals

> ### Chic Tip
>
> DO A MONTHLY CUSTOMER SPOTLIGHT OR GIVE A REWARD THAT RECOGNIZES ONE OF YOUR CUSTOMERS FOR THEIR VOLUME OF PURCHASES, THEIR UNIQUE USE OF WHAT YOU SELL, REFERRING OTHERS TO YOU, OR ANY OTHER REASON YOU CAN THINK OF TO TOOT THEIR HORN. THE REWARD CAN BE A FREE PRODUCT OR SERVICE THAT YOU SELL, A GIFT CARD FOR A STORE OR RESTAURANT, RECOGNITION IN YOUR NEWSLETTER, A PLUG FOR THEIR BUSINESS, OR INCORPORATING THEIR PICTURE IN A PHOTOMONTAGE THAT HANGS IN YOUR FRONT LOBBY—WHATEVER WOULD HAVE VALUE TO THE CUSTOMER. THE GOAL IS TO HAVE OTHER CUSTOMERS WANT TO WIN, SO MAKE THE REWARD SOMETHING THAT APPEALS TO THEM.

*qualms

*succumb

*mantra

*trepidation

and creating über successful businesses, I'm going to challenge you to do it differently. Charge a fair price, even if it is high, for what you have to sell. Do not give coupons or freebies to friends and family. And don't feel guilty! You are an entrepreneur. You work hard, and you deserve to be paid well for the unique value you have created.

What is your version of making your customer experience heaven on earth, like Benita did? No matter what kind of business you own or want to create, you can customize your products or services to include a full customer experience. The extra time you spend on the experience will pay dividends in the long run by deepening your existing customer relationships and expanding your loyal customer base. You can make the buying process easier, faster, and more comfortable. This may take money on your part and will definitely take thought, but any investment in your customers' happiness is both wise and worthwhile. Entrepreneurs often want to start a company on the cheap, and it is fine to cut corners, except when it means cutting into your customers' experience. It is not chic to look cheap.

Now, think of two ways you can make your customers' buying experiences more comfortable. To do this, take off your business owner hat for a moment and imagine what it is like to be one of your customers. Since you already have a description of your ideal customers (from Chapter Two), it will be easy for you to step into their shoes for a moment. You can visualize it in your head, or role-play with your employees, if you have them, or an impartial friend. Experiencing every interaction your customers have with your products and/or services is the way to gain much needed knowledge about them and what makes them tick. You want to be a mind reading fly on the wall when they are using your product or experiencing your service. You want to see them on the outside and hear their thoughts on the inside. Feel what they feel and see what

*Well Paid, Well Fed */ work hard so I'm well paid.

they see. You'll be amazed at how many small things you have overlooked that could make a big difference to your customers. Even though this information is of tremendous value and is so easy and inexpensive to obtain, businesses seldom spend the time to acquire it.

Get the relationship off to the right start from the beginning. When you or your employees meet a new customer, or get a call from a prospect out of the blue, are you asking, "How did you find out about us?" or "What motivated you to walk in the door?" in a friendly, caring—not interrogational—way? When talking with an existing customer, ask about their past buying experience(s), their satisfaction level, their favorite part of what you offer, and any other preferences, likes, and dislikes. What are their top priorities when they come in? Do they want expedience or would they rather feel unhurried? Determine how your company could do a better job meeting and exceeding their expectations: What additional value could you create for them, and what would they love to see you add to your mix? See if you can discern what additional value they would be willing to pay more to have. There is no need to wait to ask this formally in a survey when you can get a feeling for their value-to-price equation through good old-fashioned conversation. Think of it as a one-person focus group. How could you provide them with something that has value greater than price in their eyes and price greater than cost for you? Just like anyone seeking a relationship, customers want to feel known, loved, and appreciated. When they do, they will look forward to each interaction with your business, and they won't keep it a secret.

I love to say, "I'm going to see my hairdresser." It is rare to find one man who makes me happy every time I see him. He cuts my hair well, and we talk about what's going on in our lives, AND he gives me a diet cola and a *Vanity Fair*. He knows me. Now, that hasn't always been the case for one reason or another. People have moved. Others have gotten sloppy on the job. But because, for the most part, I know that I can expect the same consistent, positive experience from my latest hairdresser, I am loyal to him and I keep going back. I like knowing I can go to one place repeatedly for a service that I need and for an experience that I want, and your customers will like knowing that about you, too.

From a business standpoint, you will find the real value of your customers in their second and third purchases, and every one after that. You can grow the value of your business by growing the value of your customer base; in terms of business valuation, lifetime value of a customer is a more important metric than profit per sale. Even when you create a marketing campaign, you want to look at both the immediate return on investment you expect as well as the long-term customer value that you are providing.

> ### Chic Caution
>
> KNOW WHEN TO SAY WHEN. PART OF ATTRACTING IDEAL CUSTOMERS MEANS SAYING GOODBYE TO ONES WHO ARE NOT. IF A CUSTOMER BECOMES MORE TROUBLE THAN HE IS WORTH, KNOW WHEN TO LET HIM GO. A BAD CUSTOMER CAN BE A DRAIN ON YOU AND YOUR EMPLOYEES. PART OF THE JOY OF OWNING YOUR OWN COMPANY IS THAT YOU CAN CHOOSE WHOM YOU WILL SERVE. YOU DON'T HAVE TO DEAL WITH UNREASONABLE JERKS. YOU ARE IN CHARGE.

You need to put on your customers' shoes. By having an intimate knowledge of what your customers really want from your product or service or what their real pain or desire is, you will be able to create customer-driven marketing. Rather than a traditional campaign that screams ME, ME, and more about ME, a company with a customer relationship focus approaches it from the opposite angle of YOU, YOU, and everything to please YOU. As your company grows and you become more distanced from individual customer interactions, use secret shoppers. This doesn't need to be an expensive initiative, but it can yield a priceless return. Sit down and make a list of what needs to happen to create an excellent customer experience for anyone interacting with your company. Have someone test your operational process and score you on each of these criteria. Identify areas for improvement and come up with a way to implement those improvements.

Customer relationships are more profitable than transactions. When you look at the cost of acquiring a new customer versus the cost of retaining one, the mathematical conclusion is obvious: It is much cheaper to keep a customer you've already got than to go out and try to market and sell to a bunch of strangers. Instead of launching a marketing campaign that will target new customers, look into campaigns that will encourage your current customers to expand their relationships with you and warmly introduce you to a friend. You can use promotional items with your existing customers to further ingrain your brand into their lives. By keeping existing customers happy and giving them useful gifts, you effectively launch a grassroots marketing campaign simply through people toting your brand name around. Happy customers are more likely to promote you to their friends and relatives, who may well be your target customers, since birds of a feather really do tend to flock together.

It is important to pay careful attention to customer satisfaction, but perfection is not a reasonable goal, so prepare yourself and your team for service recovery situations. While it is inevitable that things will go wrong, it does not have to mean an inevitable customer defection. In fact, customers who had a good experience will tell five acquaintances, and recipients of bad service will tell ten (or more if they leverage technology), and those for whom you can turn a poor experience into a peak one will tell twenty. Realize that you will drop the ball from time to time, but if you have a plan for how to pick it back up, you can turn those fumbles into touchdowns. Without customers, you don't have a business. Keep that at the forefront of your business plan and make every effort to find and keep good customers, and your business is sure to prosper.

How Chic are You?

✦ ARE YOUR MARKETING MATERIALS WRITTEN IN YOUR LANGUAGE OR IN YOUR CUSTOMER'S LANGUAGE? ALL COMMUNICATIONS MUST KEEP THE AUDIENCE IN MIND AND READ LIKE A PRIVATE CONVERSATION TAILORED TO A SPECIFIC PERSON. IF THEY DO NOT, EVENTUALLY SOMEONE WHO SPEAKS DIRECTLY TO YOUR CUSTOMERS WILL SWAY THEM.

✦ DO YOU SPOIL YOUR CUSTOMERS? SOME COMPANIES ROLL OUT THE RED CARPET FOR THEIR CUSTOMERS; OTHERS LEAVE A BREADCRUMB TRAIL AND A DIM LIGHT BULB HANGING OVER THE DOOR. TO WHICH PLACE OF BUSINESS WOULD YOU RETURN?

✦ DO YOU KNOW YOUR CUSTOMERS BY NAME OR BY ORDER SIZE? THE PERSONAL TOUCH STARTS WITH LOOKING AT YOUR CUSTOMERS AS PEOPLE INSTEAD OF AS DOLLAR SIGNS. WHEN SERVING YOUR CUSTOMERS, REMEMBER THAT YOU ARE INDEED THERE TO SERVE THEM.

✦ WHEN CUSTOMERS COME IN, DO YOU GO OUT AND GREET THEM OR HIDE IN THE BACK? EVERYONE LIKES TO KNOW THE OWNER, SO LET THEM. DON'T HIDE BEHIND YOUR BUSINESS; LET PEOPLE SHAKE THE HAND OF THE LADY IN CHARGE.

✦ DO YOU KNOW WHO USES YOUR PRODUCT, WHO PAYS FOR IT, AND WHO INITIATES AND INFLUENCES THE DECISION TO BUY? IN AN INCREASINGLY TEAM-BASED WORK ENVIRONMENT AND NON-NUCLEAR FAMILY, THESE ARE NOT ALWAYS THE SAME PEOPLE, NOR ARE THEY THE OBVIOUS ONES. FIND OUT WHO PLAYS WHAT ROLE IN THE BUYING DECISION FROM USER TO FINANCIER TO THOSE WITH INFLUENCE AND VETO POWER, AND

MAKE SURE YOUR SALES PITCH AND YOUR CUSTOMER EXPERIENCE TAKE INTO ACCOUNT THE NEEDS AND OBJECTIVES OF EACH OF THESE PEOPLE.

DO YOU RESPOND TO ALL CUSTOMER REQUESTS WITHIN TWENTY-FOUR HOURS? FORTY-EIGHT HOURS? HAVE YOU MADE THIS GUARANTEE? RESPONSIVENESS IS A PRECURSOR TO TRUST. GETTING BACK TO PEOPLE IN A TIMELY MANNER WILL ILLUSTRATE THE VALUE AND FOCUS YOUR COMPANY PLACES ON THEM, AND SHOW THAT YOU WANT TO PLAY AN IMPORTANT ROLE IN THEIR LIVES.

DO YOU RAMBLE ON ABOUT YOUR OWN LIFE AND INSECURITIES WITHOUT EVEN REALIZING IT? THAT MAKES OTHER PEOPLE UNCOMFORTABLE. YOUR CONVERSATIONS WITH OTHERS ARE SUPPOSED TO FOCUS ON THEM, NOT ON YOU. TELL YOUR BEST FRIEND ABOUT HOW YOUR BOYFRIEND BROKE YOUR HEART AND THE EXTRA TEN POUNDS YOU'VE PACKED ON, NOT YOUR CLIENTS.

IF YOUR COMPETITORS DROPPED THEIR PRICES BY TWENTY PERCENT, WOULD ALL OF YOUR CUSTOMERS JUMP SHIP? MAKE SURE YOU ARE GIVING PEOPLE SUCH A DISTINCTIVE AND MEMORABLE EXPERIENCE THAT THEY BECOME LOYAL ENOUGH TO SEE BEYOND PRICE AND CONVENIENCE. YOU WANT CUSTOMERS TO BE WILLING TO DRIVE TWENTY MILES OUT OF THEIR WAY AND PAST FOUR OTHER ALTERNATIVES, BECAUSE THEY JUST HAVE TO USE YOU.

HOW MANY REFERRALS DID YOU GET LAST MONTH FROM EXISTING OR PAST CUSTOMERS? IF IT WAS NOT AS MANY AS YOU'D LIKE, EITHER YOU ARE NOT DELIGHTING THEM WITH YOUR SERVICE OR THEY DON'T KNOW THAT YOU WANT THEIR HELP IN SPREADING THE WORD. SO TELL THEM YOU CARE ABOUT THEIR HAPPINESS AND ASK THEM TO TELL OTHERS ABOUT YOU.

DO YOU KNOW MORE ABOUT YOUR CUSTOMERS THAN THEIR ACCOUNT NUMBERS? WHAT DO YOU THINK YOUR CUSTOMERS ARE MORE INTERESTED IN, YOUR PRODUCT OR

SERVICE OR THEIR OWN LIVES? COLLECT ALL THE DATA YOUR CUSTOMERS WILL GIVE YOU: PREFERENCES, UPCOMING LIFE EVENTS, CHALLENGES, GOALS, FAMILIES, AND TRAVELS. ORGANIZE THIS IN A CUSTOMER RELATIONSHIP MANAGEMENT (CRM) SYSTEM AND LEVERAGE THIS INSIGHT.

DO YOU RUN FROM COMPLAINTS AND BURY YOUR HEAD IN THE SAND OR EMBRACE THEM WITH OPEN ARMS? ANYTIME A CUSTOMER EXPRESSES DISSATISFACTION IS A GOLDEN OPPORTUNITY FOR YOU TO SHINE. SHOWING CUSTOMERS YOU CAN RECOVER FROM BLUNDERS WILL STRENGTHEN THEIR TRUST IN YOUR BUSINESS AND SOLIDIFY THEIR LOYALTY.

ARE YOU SELLING A ONE-SIZE-FITS-ALL SOLUTION TO CUSTOMERS OF ALL DIFFERENT SIZES? LOOK FOR WAYS YOU CAN GIVE CUSTOMERS THE POWER TO CHOSE AND CUSTOMIZE. EVERYONE LIKES TO THINK WHAT THEY'VE GOT IS ONE OF A KIND.

ARE YOU WILLING TO TAKE ANY WARM BODY AS A CUSTOMER? TRYING TO BE EVERYTHING TO EVERYONE IS NOT GOOD SERVICE; IT'S BAD BUSINESS. REMEMBER YOUR FOCUS.

CHAPTER FOUR

The DMV or Google:
Attracting and Retaining the Best Employees

Most people in America are painfully familiar with that epitome of inefficiency and bad customer experience known as the DMV[2]. The last time I went there was a total nightmare, and I swore I would never go back. I pulled into the seedy shopping center where the office is housed and looked for a parking spot, trying to avoid the potholes, oil leaks, and litter that cluttered the lot. After standing in two lines and speaking to two equally surly agents who made sure I had all the necessary paperwork, I took a ticket from the deli-counter-style machine and sat in one of fifteen rows of chairs to wait for my number—347—to flash on one of the lighted boards. They were only on 279 when I sat down, so I had plenty of time to observe the grim faces of the employees working as slowly as humanly possible, manning their desks, talking to an endless stream of people, giving eye exams, and taking pictures. I was

[2]The Department of Motor Vehicles in the United States is the commonly used name for the state government entity that handles driver's licenses and vehicle license plates. It is notorious for being slow, inefficient, and an overall unpleasant experience. This experience could be likened to going through the security line at an international airport.

51

reminded of a mob of zombies from a movie I'd seen late one night. It was a bit unnerving to think that these people have a hand in ensuring the safety and compliance of people on our roads. The attendant that I finally spoke to seemed as if she'd rather be anywhere in the world but the DMV. She was terse and seemed devoid of any happiness. I pitied her. Clearly, she hated her job.

At Google headquarters, on the other hand, employees couldn't be happier to be there, and it shows. In addition to being able to boast about working for one of the most progressive and well-known Internet brands, employees enjoy extraordinary benefits like free lunch and dinner in fabulous dining facilities, gyms, financial planning services, on-site dry cleaning, haircuts, carwashes, and commuting buses, as well as time off for child care and a vacation policy that you wouldn't even believe. Google has almost no turnover and has created a culture that advertises for them—they get piles of fresh résumés every day from applicants who have heard how well Google treats its people. These generous and creative benefits allow Google to attract the best and get the best performance possible from them.

Working for the government is a different story. Once you are in, it's hard to get fired, but without positive incentives to motivate and negative consequences to fear, employees typically do just enough to get by, leaving mediocrity as the benchmark for success. Having guaranteed employment with strong benefits seems like what all employees would want or need, until you think about the Post Office, where the term "going postal" was coined, or the DMV, where minutes can seem like hours. How would you feel if you had to do the same thing over and over again for eight hours a day, every day?

Part of what makes government and similar jobs so bad are the mind-numbing redundancies. You have to create positions for people that challenge them and allow them to use the skills they want to use. Before you became an entrepreneur, you probably had jobs that you hated, where you couldn't leverage your strengths. I know I have. Keep that in mind when you hire your employees. Even though they haven't caught the entrepreneurial bug, they still have the desire to use their talents on a daily basis and make meaningful contributions.

It's obvious why Google trumps the DMV where employees are concerned. While your small business can't offer what Google does, you can use the company's success as a guide to creating the same kind of culture people will vie to be a part of and won't want to leave. Many small businesses don't give too much thought to employees beyond hiring people when they need them, but having a well-thought-out "People Strategy" will not only save you much time and money over the years, it also could turn into a key differentiator. Employee turnover can cause huge setbacks for your business. When someone leaves, there is always lost knowledge, despite every effort to minimize what falls through the cracks in the transition. You might lose business or have to refuse work because you don't have the resources to support it. Then, of course, it takes time and money to recruit, screen, interview, and train replacement employees. Finally, you will not look as good to your customers when they start noticing new faces all the time.

Taking a proactive stance in defining your People Strategy will save you time and money in the long run.

To help you put more power in your people, ponder the following questions:

- What is your ideal business culture?
- What is the culture your ideal customers expect to see?
- What kind of culture will match your customers' style?
- How do you see your business running in five years?

53

- How do you want your employees' positions to be structured?
- Is your culture casual and laid-back or professional and regimented?
- Can you and your workforce handle the dichotomy of being casually dressed behind the scenes and professionally dressed when working with clients?
- Are your hours strictly from nine to five, or can customers call anytime? Do you expect employees to work beyond their normal schedules if need be?
- Are meetings scheduled or impromptu?
- Are your employees strictly managed or given more autonomy?
- How important is creativity in your work?
- How important are deadlines, attention to detail, and accuracy?

Once you decide what you want your company to feel like from the inside, you'll have a clear guideline for all of your human resource-related decisions. Personally, I like to maintain a good balance between the professional face that our clients see and the creative and fun atmosphere that inspires our work. I like my office to have a homey feel. I have plush couches that I encourage employees to work on when they need a break from their desks or when they are collaborating with me or other employees. Ad hoc brainstorming sessions are frequent. I don't consider myself a micro-manager, but I do check in with employees a few times throughout the day to see how their work is going and to offer feedback, ideas, and advice on dealing with challenges. Quality standards are high. Fun is encouraged in the office, but is balanced with a sense of urgency around deadlines and client satisfaction. Everyone is aware that growth is an important priority for the company, and everyone contributes to achieving that goal. Positive attitudes are another important element of our culture, and one of my criteria for hiring decisions. Everyone in my company displays positive thinking and optimism. From a décor standpoint, I like to have brightly painted walls, artwork that inspires creativity, and shelves full of books that promote learning. These are all, of course, personal preferences, but they are decisions that I made to create a company with

> **— Chic Tip —**
>
> ENCOURAGE PLAY. IN ORDER TO INSPIRE GENIUS AT WORK, IT IS IMPORTANT TO CREATE A CULTURE THAT INCLUDES AN ELEMENT OF PLAY. PROVIDE A PLAYFUL ENVIRONMENT WITH GAMES LIKE NERF BASKETBALL, A BEST HALLOWEEN COSTUME CONTEST, AND A JOKE-OF-THE-DAY OR CARTOON-OF-THE-WEEK BOARD.

the culture that I desired. What type of culture will allow you to provide unique value to the marketplace and make your employees and your customers feel a personal connection?

Your business starts as an extension of yourself; so make sure that you, first and foremost, are comfortable and inspired. From there, find out what resonates most with your customers: What do they like most about doing business with you? Look to replicate that experience by building those elements into your employee culture. This assures that your whole company is portraying one consistent personality—one your customers will come to know you by and love.

How Can You Find the Right Employees for Your Business's Culture?

Finding your first employee or your fiftieth can be an arduous task that can lead to either a long-lasting, mutually beneficial relationship or a short-lived, disastrous debacle. No one can predict the future, but you can do certain things to ensure that you are choosing the best candidate possible for every open position.

Decide from the beginning that you only want top talent working for you. To build a great company, you need great people.

One way to find candidates is to ask for referrals from trusted friends and colleagues. Starting a relationship through a mutual acquaintance facilitates initial trust and rapport building; however, the weakness of this method is that you are limited to whom you know and whom they know. You might not be able to find enough good people or the particular degrees or skill sets that you need. Unless you happen to be lucky enough to trip right over a dream applicant (which does happen from time to time if you set a strong enough intention), you probably need a supplementary approach.

> ### Chic Tip
>
> OFFER CREATIVE BENEFITS LIKE HALF-DAY FRIDAYS, FLEXIBLE WORK SCHEDULES, OR THE ABILITY TO VACATION FOR MORE THAN TWO WEEKS (PAID OR UNPAID, DEPENDING ON WHAT YOU CAN AFFORD). APPRENTICESHIPS IN AN AREA OF INTEREST, THE CHANCE TO EXPERIMENT WITH GROUNDBREAKING INNOVATION OR AN OPPORTUNITY TO TAKE ON A GREATER LEADERSHIP ROLES ARE ALSO CARROTS YOU CAN DANGLE TO HELP YOU ATTRACT AND RETAIN TOP TALENT. BECAUSE YOUR HANDS ARE NOT TIED WITH THE ROPES OF BUREAUCRACY, YOU CAN GIVE EMPLOYEES THINGS THE BIG COMPANIES CANNOT.

I suggest you use word-of-mouth, online networking sites, free job-search websites, local colleges and universities, community bulletin boards, relevant blogs, social networking sites, and your own website to find the talent pool you need. Newspapers and sites like Monster and CareerBuilder are probably not your best bet: The cost can be prohibitive for a small company, and the effectiveness is not guaranteed. You might reap a high volume of applicants, but remember that you are looking for quality and fit, not quantity. People searching the big sites are usually looking for jobs with established companies that offer a market-rate salary and benefits. Unless you are prepared to meet these expectations, you could waste a lot of time sifting through qualified people who, unfortunately, are not a match for your company. Secondly, those with the time to surf these big job boards and have no qualms about posting their resumes on them are likely not working, so you have to wonder why that is. On the other hand, sites like Craigslist allow you to post a job for free (in most areas) and attract highly qualified people who desire to do something a bit different and tend to have more flexible requirements. Mentioning that your company is growing and you are always looking for great people is another free tactic for collecting names to put into the pool. Start a "job candidate" folder and fill it with business cards of people you meet or get introduced to who you think would make a good addition to your team.

Taking on a full-time employee is a big commitment, so make sure you know what you can afford. One option is to start new employees off part time and give it a month or two to make sure that your demand will continue to enable you to support their salaries. Since many people looking for permanent positions are not willing to accept part-time work, you can turn to schools and their websites for not only part-time employees, but also interns (who might even work for free). Interns and more conventional part-time help are often good options for small firms that need to make sure the increased overhead

> ### Chic Tip
>
> DELEGATE WHILE MAINTAINING VISIBILITY. HAVE EMPLOYEES CC OR BCC YOU (OR THEIR DIRECT MANAGER) ON CLIENT CORRESPONDENCE AND SIT IN ON MEETINGS AND CALLS PERIODICALLY TO KEEP TABS ON HOW THINGS ARE GOING. YOU BROUGHT EMPLOYEES IN TO TAKE THE WORK OFF YOUR SHOULDERS, BUT REMEMBER THAT YOU ARE ULTIMATELY THE ONE ACCOUNTABLE FOR EVERYTHING IN YOUR CHIC COMPANY.

that comes with hiring is covered by a relatively immediate corresponding increase in revenue.

One thing to remember when hiring is that you are in control of the search; you are not backed up against a wall even if you feel like it. Barring having that perfect candidate's résumé fall into your lap through a referral or a miracle, most hiring decisions take time. You might feel you are desperate to find someone as soon as possible, but it is a lot more expensive and troublesome to hire the wrong person than to have the position remain open. By starting early and exercising patience, you can find great employees who will love your business almost as much as you do.

I have had clients who convinced themselves they needed to find an employee immediately so they looked over a few résumés and picked out the best one in order to get someone into their office fast. This is a mistake in any kind of market. Finding an employee quickly doesn't mean you have to limit yourself to the first résumés that come in. You can avoid this situation by developing an operational plan for the next twelve months. Draft an organizational chart of what you would like your company to look like. By understanding what your future needs will be, you can preemptively get ready for new employees and avoid succumbing to the temptation of quick fix desperate hiring. Whether you review submitted résumés or use referrals, have an initial pool of at least three qualified candidates for each spot. To expedite the hiring process, you or one of your employees with more downtime can pre-screen candidates through quick phone interviews or emails.

One necessary pre-screening question is, "What is your salary range?" Many candidates don't want to ask about salary because they are worried about sounding too preoccupied with money, but if your salary range does not match their needs, they will not accept the position, no matter what. Thus, I believe it is better to discuss salary up front to ensure that everyone is on the same page and no one's time is wasted. In my opinion, it is far better practice to weed people out at the beginning than to go through the entire interview process only to have your favorite candidate be disappointed with the salary. If salary is dependent on experience, tell the candidate what the salary range is and how the experience correlates. Don't put yourself in a position where you are tempted to hire someone you can't afford. Set the right parameters up front and you'll find good employees for the salary you can pay.

The way to attract great people is by creating a great job, and a great job does not necessarily mean a huge paycheck. While always a factor, money is just one of many important elements that people consider. People are looking to be part of something. Similar to how customers are searching for emotional fulfillment in their purchases, more and more employees are searching for purpose

Chic Tip

GO TO GOOGLE'S CORPORATE WEBSITE AND PICK JUST ONE BENEFIT THAT YOU CAN OFFER YOUR EMPLOYEES.

in their work. Since people spend so much of their lives at work, many are realizing that job satisfaction is just as much a requirement as decent pay. Employees want to feel that their efforts are valued and going toward some greater good that makes the world better, even if it is just in some small way.

Most of the job candidates you want are likely to be working for someone else already, so it is important to have a strategy that goes beyond a wing and a prayer for attracting them. Since you might not be able to offer the dream salary and benefit package from the beginning, you'll have to think beyond money to make the job you are offering great. Don't let this dishearten you; this is simply another opportunity to be creative. There are loads of people out there who are fed up with working obscene and undervalued hours in cubicle hell for a large corporation and would willingly sacrifice pay for things like power, autonomy, flexibility, more vacation time, rewards tied to performance, and a feeling of purpose and connection. Fortunately, those are exactly the types of things you have to offer that the big guys don't.

When you bring a candidate in to interview, be sure to start the meeting with casual conversation, to make the candidate comfortable and relaxed. I have interviewed enough people to know that successful hires are usually ones who cannot only answer business questions on the spot, but can also hold a conversation. Casual conversation is also an effective way to get the candidate to share things that you can't ask about, such as marital status, children, age, and future life plans. Once you have broken the ice, move into the interview questions. Depending on the position, your questions might center on skills and experience, or thinking and behavior. It is a good idea to find out a bit about both, so include a mixture of "How many times have you done X?" and "Describe a situation where you encountered a problem at work and solved it." Make sure there is enough back-and-forth dialogue to give you a sense of how the person thinks. Remember, you are hiring a person, not a robot, and whomever you hire will have their own life, personality, values, and issues that they will bring to your company every day.

If you are clicking with a candidate, have someone else meet with them to give their assessment. Having a strong personal

> ## Chic Exercise
>
> TAKE OUT A PIECE OF PAPER AND FOLD IT VERTICALLY DOWN THE MIDDLE. ON ONE SIDE, JOT DOWN AT LEAST TEN THINGS THAT SOMEONE WOULD LOVE ABOUT WORKING FOR YOU. ON THE OTHER SIDE, LIST WHAT YOU THINK ARE SOME OF THE BIG NEGATIVES. SEE IF YOU CAN FLIP THE NEGATIVES INTO POSITIVES, AND WRITE DOWN MORE POSITIVES IN YOUR PRO COLUMN. NOW THAT YOU HAVE A CLEAR SENSE OF WHAT THE TRADEOFF LOOKS LIKE, YOU CAN SPEAK ABOUT IT OPENLY WITH YOUR CANDIDATES TO GIVE THEM A CLEAR SENSE OF WHAT YOU ARE OFFERING. YOUR IDEAL EMPLOYEES WILL BE THOSE FOR WHOM THE PROS OUTWEIGH THE CONS.

connection with someone up front can leave you blind to other faults or potential issues. It is important to get a second opinion. If there is no one else at your office, you might want to have another conversation with the candidate or get a work sample to make sure that they are the right fit for your business. You could also ask a friend or business consultant to spend a few minutes on the phone with the candidate.

> **Chic Tip**
>
> TAKE ALL JOB CANDIDATES WHO WILL INTERACT WITH CUSTOMERS OUT FOR A MEAL TO ASSESS THEIR DINING ETIQUETTE. REMEMBER, THIS PERSON IS GOING TO BE REPRESENTING YOU TO THE WORLD. MAKING SURE THEY WERE NOT RAISED BY WOLVES IS WORTH THE PRICE OF LUNCH.

Immediately after an interview, sit down with a notepad, write the person's name on a piece of paper, and describe who they are. Jot down what you learned and how you felt about this candidate. Make sure you take at least five minutes between interviews or before starting something else to write down your thoughts; it is easy to forget how you felt or whom you liked as time passes.

Some questions to ask yourself about candidates are:
- How did I feel about our interaction?
- Did we click?
- Does this person seem to have a strong work ethic?
- Do they have the right background and skill set?
- Do they seem like someone who will thrive in my business?
- Do both their work history and current circumstances indicate that they will stay in this business/with my company for the foreseeable future?

After an interview, always make sure that you ask for references (for schools and/or positions held) and take the time to check them. Unfortunately, a piece of paper (even a letter of reference) is not enough proof that a person is who they say they are.

You want to make sure that you spend enough time choosing the right person for the job. Finding the right fit for your business is never going to be quick and easy; there are too many factors to consider. Once you have gathered all the data you can, in the end you are going to have to go with your gut feeling, or women's intuition. If you clicked with the candidate, did your homework, and feel excited about what the person can do for the company, the likelihood of your keeping and being happy with this new employee is high.

Starting off Right

Chic Caution

DON'T PEER OVER EMPLOYEES' SHOULDERS, OR MAKE THEM FEEL LIKE YOU ARE WATCHING THEM LIKE A HAWK, ESPECIALLY IF YOUR OFFICE QUARTERS ARE SOMEWHAT COZY (A.K.A. SMALL). IT'S IMPORTANT TO GIVE YOUR EMPLOYEES A CERTAIN LEVEL OF PRIVACY. REALIZE THAT YOU ARE THE BOSS AND CARRY AN INTIMIDATION FACTOR (EVEN IF YOU DON'T FEEL THAT WAY). DON'T CREATE AN OPPRESSIVE ENVIRONMENT WHERE EMPLOYEES FEEL THEY CAN'T MAKE A PERSONAL PHONE CALL OR CHECK THEIR PERSONAL EMAIL. AS LONG AS THEY ARE GETTING THEIR WORK DONE, ALLOW THEM THE AUTONOMY SOMEONE AT THEIR LEVEL DESERVES.

Orientation is a must for all new hires, even your very first employee. There are many things about your company that you might assume would be obvious to anyone, but this is not the time to take anything for granted. Even if your business has developed very informally up until now, employees are best brought on through a structured process. This on-boarding process should include an overview of your company and its customers, processes, and culture, as well as the employee's roles, responsibilities, and clearly specified objectives. You probably talked about the history of the company during the interview, but the employee was most likely a tad nervous and more intent on what to say next. So, now is the time to tell them about your grand vision and re-sell them on the great company you've created and the great opportunity you have given them. Getting employees excited in the first week is critical for the long-term success of the relationship.

You Have a Good Employee, Now What?

You want your employees to grow and develop along with your company so that they can get better at what they do and ultimately take on more responsibility. The more you develop people, the more profitable they will become for the company. To keep them on the track of continuous improvement, set up a rolling performance-enhancement plan for the year. Look at developing three skills related to job performance for every employee, every year. Brainstorm with your employees concerning ways they can or want to improve, and have them spend four months focusing on getting stronger in one of these areas. At the end of each four-month period, you can discuss the challenges and successes they experienced and then have them move on to the next skill. Have a career conversation with every employee at least once a year. Whether your employees plan to spend the rest of their careers with

> ### Chic Tip
>
> GIVE EMPLOYEES A LEARNING AND DEVELOPMENT BUDGET. IF YOUR BUDGET IS SMALL, IT COULD BE AS SIMPLE AS TWENTY DOLLARS FOR THE BOOK OF THEIR CHOICE TO STRENGTHEN A SKILL OR LEARN SOMETHING NEW. WHEN YOU'VE GOT A BIT MORE TO INVEST IN YOUR PEOPLE, THEIR TRAINING BUDGET COULD BE A STIPEND FOR A CLASS OR SEMINAR. THIS IS A GREAT WAY TO CREATE A CULTURE OF CONTINUOUS IMPROVEMENT AND SHOWS YOUR EMPLOYEES THAT YOU WANT TO CREATE A LEARNING ORGANIZATION AND ARE WILLING TO INVEST IN THEM AS THE VALUABLE ASSETS THEY ARE.

you or not, you'll get the best performance out of them if you help them reach their ultimate career objectives. The more time you spend talking to your employees, the more likely that their true aspirations will come out. If you can tie your employees' jobs to one of their big personal or professional goals, you'll find they will bring their best efforts to the table for you. These career conversations might also lead you to discover additional skills that employees could use to benefit your company.

Once you have gotten good people to come work for you, you must keep them on your side by keeping them engaged and in the loop. The sad fact is that nearly three-quarters of all employees are looking for another job[3]. Make sure your employees know what is

> **Chic Tip**
>
> TIE AN END-OF-YEAR BONUS TO A COLLECTIVE GOAL THAT EVERYONE HAS A HAND IN, LIKE CUSTOMER RETENTION RATES. COLLECTIVE GOALS STIMULATE TEAMWORK, WHICH ALL ORGANIZATIONS NEED IN ORDER TO WIN.

expected of them and how their roles fit into the great goal of the company. Having a vision and values that get your employees excited can be just as motivational as money. To make sure that they really feel like they are part of the team, communicate with them. Share the goals of the company with them and let them know the particulars of the business, such as revenue and expenses. Obviously, it is not appropriate to share every line item with them, but if you want them to have an impact on the top and bottom lines, it is important for them to understand the operational costs of the company as well as the revenue drivers and desired and actual results.

It is great fun to develop and grow people. The less fun side of human resources is having to let someone go, but just like every other challenge of running a business, you can handle this, too. If someone is not performing at the level you want, you need to do something about it right away. Let them know that you are concerned about their performance and put together a thirty-day

---

[3] According to a 2006 US Job Retention Poll by the Society of Human Resource Management (SHIRM) and the Wall Street Journal's CareerJournal.com and Yahoo's Hotjobs.

improvement plan, with milestones that you want to see achieved along the way. Make sure you have them sign a document acknowledging that you had this conversation. Observe their performance, get feedback from others, and hold regular meetings with the employee to assess if improvement is indeed taking place. Sometimes people improve and sometimes they don't. Remember: You are running a business. Hiring and firing are business decisions, not personal ones. One of the biggest mistakes small business owners make is keeping bad people for too long. So, once you realize someone is not going to be a good fit, don't wait. Professionally and politely inform them this is not going to work out and you wish them the best in their future endeavors. Consult an attorney or HR expert to make sure that you comply with all legalities.

Consider This...

A person's job is closely tied to their self-esteem. Thus, your employees' titles deserve careful consideration. Titles are important. People use them to tell other people what they do. People internalize titles and incorporate them into their own self-identity. It is my belief that if you give someone a good title, they will live up to it. There is a difference between being a *Supervisor* and being the *Vice President of Customer Satisfaction*. Instead of arbitrarily assigning titles to jobs, discuss what title your employee feels comfortable having.

> **Chic Tip**
>
> COME UP WITH INEXPENSIVE WAYS TO RECOGNIZE EMPLOYEES FOR GOING ABOVE AND BEYOND, LIKE TEMPORARILY DESIGNATING THE BEST PARKING SPOT FOR THEM, POSTING THEIR NAME AND PICTURE AS "EMPLOYEE OF THE MONTH," OR CREATING A FANCY OR FUNNY TROPHY OR PLAQUE THAT SITS ON THEIR DESK FOR THE MONTH.

Give them options. If you are going to take the time and money to make business cards for your employees, give them titles that they will be proud of and make them feel invested. That'll get them passing those business cards around.

Meet Sarah and Seema

Sarah and Seema are two entrepreneurs whose differing employee strategies will give you a taste of what managing people is all about.

Sarah owns a web design company, WebWorks, which she started out of her home. At first, Sarah did custom design jobs herself, but as she found new business, she knew she needed to stay in front of prospects and clients and hire others to do the project work. Because she wanted to pay lower-end salaries, she decided to hire students right out of college with computer and graphic design degrees.

Initially, employees worked in Sarah's spare bedroom, and she made sure to give them regular raises and benefits. She grew her workforce up to ten employees, seven of whom worked from home. After ten years in business, Sarah realized that her employees usually stayed with her only two years before moving on to something else. They often quit with little warning, many times leaving Sarah high and dry mid-project. Sarah was puzzled by this trend and knew that the turnover was contributing to her stagnant profits.

All of her employees worked forty hours a week and enjoyed good pay and benefits, with standard raises. Sarah thought that she was running a first-rate business that any employee would be grateful to be a part of. Her employees showed no signs of unhappiness. They were always nice to her in the office, on the telephone, and over email, so she couldn't imagine why they were perpetually leaving. Despite the pleasantries, underneath the surface, Sarah's employees felt under-appreciated, had no sense of belonging, and were frustrated by the lack of a reward system. Some of Sarah's designers were fast and could design three websites in a week, and others could only design one site a week, but there were no processes or incentives in place to reward, or even recognize, the efficient employees for their productivity. With no incentive to be faster or more creative, employees became de-motivated. They began to work less and surf the Internet more and became less invested in the business and its success.

Additionally, office politics had become an issue, with employees increasingly frustrated and annoyed by their co-workers. Since there were no face-to-face team meetings or employee get-togethers, Sarah's employees didn't know each other well, a situation that was exacerbated by the fact that employees mostly emailed each other to accomplish tasks. There was a great deal of miscommunication and negative interpretation; people felt that their co-workers had sent them rude emails or given them incomplete information. Over time, these feelings of frustration and an-

> **Chic Tip**
>
> TALK TO EVERYONE ON YOUR TEAM EVERY WEEK ABOUT HIS OR HER PERFORMANCE. IF THEY ARE TOP PERFORMERS, TELL THEM WHAT THEY DO THAT MAKES A DIFFERENCE AND WHY. IF THEY COULD USE SOME IMPROVEMENT, TELL THEM WHAT THEY NEED TO DO TO MAKE EVEN MORE OF A POSITIVE IMPACT IN THEIR ROLE AND WHY. CHALLENGE EACH PERSON TO CONTINUE TO REDEFINE HIS OR HER OWN PERSONAL BEST AT WORK EVERY DAY.

noyance turned to apathy, and employees who had once been thrilled to be able to work from home felt out of the loop entirely.

The disjointed nature of Sarah's office led to a disconnected culture. While Sarah's compensation packages were generous, she failed to offer incentives to bring the best out of her employees. Miscommunication also caused employees to feel detached and even aggravated with one another. Since Sarah never took the time to discuss career plans with any of her employees, it was not surprising that they never really saw a future there; once they got bored, they simply went elsewhere to develop and grow, without a twinge of sadness about leaving WebWorks behind.

Now meet Seema, who has fulfilled her lifelong dream of owning an independent bookstore. She had worked as a textbook inventory manager for a university bookstore for twelve years, during which time she saved money and took the time to plan and write down what she wanted her store to be like. She loved independent bookstores where employees recommended their personal picks and made customers feel at home in the store.

Seema decided that her store, The Book Shelf, would be the kind of neighborhood store that had quarterly book signings with local authors. To get her employees to feel like part of the team, she decided to give each one the responsibility of organizing one book signing a year. This not only made them vested in the success of the event, but also took that responsibility off Seema's shoulders and allowed her focus to remain on the big picture of running the business. When she interviewed potential employees, Seema made sure to ask them about their favorite local authors and told them about her book-signing program. When new employees started, Seema assigned a book signing to each one, along with a copy of the author's most recent book to read. Employees got excited about their authors and would brainstorm amongst themselves, regular customers, and their friends about how to promote their upcoming book signing in the community. It became a source of camaraderie for the whole team.

Seema also encouraged her employees to read if they were caught up on their work and no customers were in the store, so her staff could become more informed about the products they were selling. During their monthly team meetings, all employees came in ready to discuss the business and suggest improvements. At each meeting, Seema invited one employee to speak briefly about a book they had recently read. She allowed up to fifteen minutes for a question-and-answer session among the group. This made everyone better salespeople, and her employees began lobbying to get to speak at the monthly meeting.

Seema did experience employee turnover. One person she hired had aspirations of becoming an author. Knowing that he would not be a career employee, Seema only asked him to work hard and let her know of his plans. She tried to give him projects that would interest him and help him reach his goals. Seema treated the employee fairly, and he, in turn, made sure to give ample notice before leaving. He also recommended one of his female friends as a potential employee. Seema interviewed the girl, liked her, and ended up hiring her. By discussing her employee's aspirations in the open, Seema not only made a smooth transition, but she also got her former employee to agree to come back and do a signing in her store.

Seema had another employee who continually sat by the cash register reading. She first encouraged him to spend more time with the customers, but his shyness persisted. After considering her employee's skills, Seema met with him and recommended that he find work at a library, where sales skills were not needed. Seema told him that she would be a good reference, and within three weeks, the employee had a new job, but he still returned to shop at Seema's bookstore.

Over the years, The Book Shelf has become what Seema wanted it to be: a prosperous store, connected to the neighborhood, with employees who are emotionally invested in the success of the store and as much a part of the unique value The Book Shelf provides to customers as Seema is.

How Can You Be More Like Seema?

Two heads are better than one; that's why you bring on employees in the first place. Building a strong team is an essential part of building a business. Once you understand what you are best at and what the market values, augment your skills with those of others. While some people start a business just to create jobs for themselves, a true business is about creating synergy—a whole that is greater than the sum of its parts. You do this by involving other people and their various insights and input; these people will be the building blocks of your company.

Create great jobs that keep employees engaged and allow them to reach their own goals by striving for yours. Be selective during your interview process. Hire self-motivated people who will do their best and want to learn and grow and serve customers. You don't want to have to tell people what to do all the time; you want employees who have an inner drive to produce results and can think and take initiative on their own. Give all of your employees the opportunity to succeed, regardless of background. Let go of preconceived notions regarding age, gender, or any other factors. Make your organization one in which performance speaks for itself. Set goals for performance and hold people accountable to them. Provide and encourage regular training and continued learning. By making your employees better, you'll make your company better. Remember that growing a business can be fun, and people who are having fun do a better job. Make having fun part

> ## Chic Tip
>
> ASK YOUR EMPLOYEES HOW THEY DO THEIR BEST WORK. DO THEY NEED TOTAL SILENCE AND SOLITUDE, THE HUM OF ACTIVITY, OR A FUN TEAM ENVIRONMENT? GIVE THEM THE ENVIRONMENT THEY NEED TO FLOURISH BY DOING THINGS LIKE PLAYING MUSIC IN THE OFFICE TO SPUR CREATIVITY; SUPPLYING CAFFEINE, CHOCO-LATE, OR HEALTHY SNACKS; OR ALLOWING THEM TO WORK FROM HOME AT TIMES.

of your culture and create a shared ownership mentality.

By constantly evaluating your employees' performance and motivations, and considering your customers' needs, your own management style, and the company culture, you can be a Google, too.

How Chic are You?

Do your employees look happy to be showing up at your office? Sober? Employees are the most under-tapped asset in business. Get more value out of yours by helping them to choose to bring their best selves to the table every day.

Are you happy to be showing up at your office? You want to create a job that you will love, not one that you dread. Make sure you are spending most of your time doing what you are best at and what you love most.

Do people need to ask for your permission or get your approval on everything? Your mission and culture need to be clear enough to guide the majority of the day-to-day actions of your team.

How did last year's performance reviews go? Did you do them? Whether your process is formal or informal, your employees deserve to have you recognize the good, find areas that they can improve on, and coach them to bring out their best

Do employees act like adults or do they fight with each other or throw tantrums? Have you laid down the laws of the land? Perhaps a policy and procedures manual is necessary, or a code of conduct.

71

◢ DID YOU HAVE A HOLIDAY PARTY LAST YEAR OR A SUMMER PICNIC? PEOPLE WANT TO FEEL THEY ARE PART OF SOMETHING. AS AN EMPLOYER, YOUR JOB IS TO MAKE YOUR EMPLOYEES FEEL THEY ARE PART OF YOUR COMPANY. SOCIAL RITUAL DONE WELL IS A HIGHLY EFFECTIVE WAY TO ACCOMPLISH THAT.

◢ CAN YOU WALK THROUGH YOUR OFFICE WITHOUT TRIPPING? CAN OTHER PEOPLE? EXTENSION CORDS ARE NOT EVEN SUPPOSED TO BE VISIBLE, MUCH LESS AN IMPEDIMENT. ELIMINATE SAFETY HAZARDS FOR YOURSELF AND YOUR TEAM.

◢ IS YOUR ORGANIZATION A DICTATORSHIP OR A DEMOCRACY? PEOPLE WILL SUPPORT THAT WHICH THEY HAVE A HAND IN CREATING, SO ALLOW THEM TO TAKE OWNERSHIP AND YOU'LL SEE THEIR CONTRIBUTIONS SOAR.

◢ DO YOU AND YOUR STAFF BEHAVE DIFFERENTLY WHEN YOU ARE IN FRONT OF A CUSTOMER? JUST AS AN ACTOR PUTTING ON A PLAY, WHEN YOU ARE ON STAGE, YOU MUST DELIVER THE PERFORMANCE YOUR PAYING GUESTS DESERVE.

CHAPTER FIVE

Delta or Microsoft: Do You Know Your Cash Flow?

Fitting its name, Delta Airlines has seen a lot of change over the last decade. In the wake of falling demand for air travel coupled with a spike in jet fuel prices, Delta and several other airlines have faced cash crises that have led to bankruptcy and spurred hostile takeover attempts. The airlines' challenge is that they have high fixed costs, both in terms of capital investment in million-dollar planes and the labor and fuel costs per trip. If they can't fill the planes, they are losing money. Due to the importance of the load factor (percentage of seats sold), airlines will play all kinds of pricing games to maximize butts in seats. Over time, however, this practice has backfired, as it has commoditized their service. While frequent flyer programs have created some loyalty, even those programs have essentially been commoditized, as cost cutting has eroded every aspect of the customer experience. With perceived value down, and fare comparison data readily available on the information superhighway, large hub and spoke carriers lost their pricing power and thus their ability to control their top line.

Reductions in travel budgets, coupled with increased hassle and lower service levels, have left many business travelers exploring conference calls, web meetings, and video conferencing as substitutes. Lucky for Delta, its hub is located in what has become one of the busiest airports in the world; therefore, despite a reputation for lackluster customer service, many customers must fly Delta by default, just to get where they want to go. It will be interesting to see how much longer Delta can survive.

Admittedly, the airline industry has one of the toughest business models to crack, but carriers like AirTran and Southwest have managed to grow and thrive by minimizing frills and ticket prices, maximizing their utilization of assets, and keeping operations simple while still delivering a personal customer experience. As a niche player, Southwest does not offer first-class seating, meals, or posh airport VIP clubs, but their employees share a culture of cooperation that makes them more productive. Southwest turns planes around at record speeds, an efficiency it has achieved by cross-training employees. Southwest also realized that having a great experience doesn't have to mean huge cash outlays; jokes are free, and they are also the thing you hear about most when people talk about a trip on Southwest. With funny flight attendants and limited routes, they are able to do more by doing less. By being lean and focused and adding value with a humorous touch, Southwest has managed to profit each year in the same high-fixed-cost industry that has choked Delta and other airlines (some to death). By making sure every dollar spent is earning a return, Southwest made the airline business model work for it.

Chic Entrepreneurs know that adding value and creating a delightful customer experience doesn't always take cash. By understanding your business model, and learning to read your financials and do predictive analysis, you can keep your cash flow in check so you don't become a Delta.

Microsoft's business model is a different story. While the company incurs heavy research and development (R&D) costs creating innovative software, once it takes a product to market, every sale is practically pure revenue. Microsoft has maintained a strong cash position by spreading overhead across a huge sales volume with low variable costs, especially now that buyers can download products off the Internet. Compare that to the cost of flying a Boeing 767.

From the beginning, Microsoft built a business by selling relatively inexpensive software that millions of customers could use without extensive training, services, or support. An important element of the Microsoft business model is protecting intellectual property in order to reap benefits from widespread use of the technology created. Software businesses spend a lot of money on R&D before they get any return. This process can take years, but once the product is ready, it can be licensed to yield high-margin revenue in market after market.

A Chic Entrepreneur knows that for any business model to work, she must pick the right market, build the right product, and be able to survive until the market is ready, which means carefully managing every penny. The cash you have must last until you start making money or can attract money from somewhere else. Neither Microsoft nor Apple began in Class A office space, but rather in a dorm room and a garage, respectively. Many dotcoms, on the other hand, played this business model wrong at the turn of the century, when they spent huge amounts of money advertising free services that yielded no revenue. They burned through all their venture capital and never made any money. Minimize your initial overhead and make sure your business model is both profitable and scalable, so that each additional sale is actually netting you more profit.

Today, Microsoft's software powers more than ninety percent of all the world's personal computers. Although Google and other open source technologies are now threatening this monopoly, no one is too worried about Microsoft, because the company has the cash to defend its position and adapt to an ever-changing industry. Having cash in your business purse will give you staying power and strength in a competitive market.

What Can You Learn From
These Two Companies?

Your sales and cost figures may have a few less zeros in them than these companies, but even if your numbers are currently at zero, you still need to know where every dime is going and what the return on investment of every dollar is. A Chic Entrepreneur knows she needs to understand her business model. Few entrepreneurs start a business just to have the pleasure of poring over financial statements, organizing receipts, and tinkering with Excel spreadsheets to optimize the numbers, but disciplined financial management is what sets apart the sissies from the women. Analyzing financials may not be your idea of fun or glamour, but it is a critical aspect of being the CEO of your dream.

Unfortunately, the aspect of business most often overlooked by women is the financial side. While I don't subscribe to the stereotypical notion that the extent of most women's money know-how is confined to how to spend it, I do think there are some money issues we face as a gender. Cash-flow management is the cold, often frustrating part of the business, and many women would prefer to engulf themselves in more of the warm and fuzzy. Like it or not, money is the language of business, so you need to learn to talk the talk and cuddle up and get comfortable with your cash, even if it isn't all that pretty right now.

A profitable business model means that after you pay every bill and everyone (including yourself), there is still money left over. To create this, you must know your fixed costs, which you will incur whether you sell anything or not, and understand your variable costs, which go into creating what you sell.

Many people set their sights too low—like just breaking even. Being able to pay the bills at the end of the month is great, but you need a loftier goal. If you just want to make enough money to get by, you're not Chic Entrepreneur material. A Chic Entrepreneur is not satisfied with low expectations. If you want to make a profit and are willing to do the legwork it takes to figure out the financials, you can be a Microsoft.

How Can You Increase Your Cash Position?

Whether you have money or you don't, it's important to get good at cash management. There are two ways to get money: earn it or get others to give it to you. You will likely use a combination of these two approaches throughout your business lifecycle, and understanding the basics of good cash-flow management will help you use both in the wisest way possible. By using aggressive cash-management strategies, you can improve cash flow internally and reduce the need to look for outside money.

Start by creating a budget. If you were in business last year or prior, you have numbers for how much you brought in and how much you spent. This is a perfect starting point.

Break your expenses into categories that make sense, and answer the following questions:

- How much did you spend on rent, utilities, office supplies, materials, marketing, etc.?
- What percentage of your costs went to each category and does that make sense?

- What did you buy that was worth it?
- What did you buy that was not?
- Are there areas where you think you should be spending more money?
- If you are not sure, this would be a good discussion to have with your accountant.

Next, figure out where most of your revenue came from:

- What are your biggest-selling items or who are your highest-dollar clients?
- How much do you sell of product A, B, and C?
- Which products/services yield the highest profit margins?

Use this data to start filling in monthly projections on an income statement for the coming year (if you don't have an income statement template, you can readily find one on the Internet). Ideally, there would be an upward trend over time, but make sure your numbers tally with what your realistic expectations are. Good cash-flow management is about thinking in terms of the future and predicting how much your business will make and what you will have to spend to make it happen. Setting a realistic revenue goal is important, especially if it feels uncomfortable, because it will give you focus and perspective.

It Is Not Just About the Cash;
It's Also About the *Flow*

It is not enough just to have a big pile of money. Money needs to be moving—circulating through the veins of the business. To increase your flow, look for "cash clogs" in the business and find ways to clear them. Is your cash tied up in excess supplies, piles of orders that are waiting to ship, or returned or damaged goods? Do you have to pay people to stand idle when there is no work coming in?

Common ways to free up cash are reducing inventory or work in progress, slowing down payables, and speeding up receivables. Your goal is to get supply to match demand as closely as possible, while still being able to meet expected delivery times. You want to pay for everything that goes into your product or service, including labor, as slowly as possible and collect what you get from the sale of it as quickly as possible. Once you get cash, keep a tight grip on it. Timing is everything. Stretch out paying bills until you absolutely must. See if you can negotiate terms that are more favorable with vendors and suppliers by giving them something of value, like a testimonial, case study, or an exclusive commitment, or offer to share your sales forecast in order to more closely tie your supply chains. Many vendors will give you 60-, 90-, or even 120-day terms if you ask. Remember, these vendors are people who are trying to sell to you. They want your business, so you can dictate the terms that you require in exchange for giving it to them. By slowing down cash outflows, you can keep the cash in your account longer.

The other side of the cash-flow equation involves speeding up your cash inflows by collecting from customers sooner. One mistake I see many small business owners make is offering terms and being paid (or not paid!) *after* a product or service is rendered. Why would you do this? Why not get paid up front? Think about a grocery store: Do they give you thirty-day terms? Of course not! If you want that food, you have to pay for it right then and there. Why can't your collections model be the same? Instead of billing people, get your money when you deliver the

Chic Tip

ACCEPT CREDIT CARDS. FIND A MERCHANT SERVICES PROVIDER TO QUOTE YOU SOME RATES. SINCE MOST PEOPLE THESE DAYS MAKE THE MAJORITY OF THEIR PURCHASES WITH CREDIT CARDS, MAKE IT EASIER FOR THEM TO GIVE YOU THEIR MONEY. MOST PEOPLE ARE ALSO LESS PRICE SENSITIVE WHEN THEY KNOW THEY CAN CHARGE IT AND THEY ALSO TEND TO BUY MORE.

product. If you are in a services business, you can ask for full or partial payment up front, or at the very least, bill immediately upon service completion. You'll be surprised how many people will write you a check or give you a credit card number on the spot, without a second thought. However, by waiting two weeks after the work is done to send an invoice with thirty-day terms, you create your own cash crunch. Another trick I've learned is to give a discount if clients pay within ten days. This is a great way to get money in the door fast. You can even build this "discount" into your pricing structure, so that you end up making the same, and getting it a lot sooner.

Be the toughest vendor your customers have; demand payment up front or right away, and don't be afraid to hound people for money past due. Many small business owners fear this will make them look weak or like they are strapped for cash, but there is nothing wrong with asking for money that is owed to you; in fact, it's irresponsible not to. Stay on top of your receivables. Call the day the payment was supposed to arrive and did not. Train your customers to know that call is coming and, in turn, you will train them to pay on time. Build policies around getting cash sooner and paying it out later, and you can buy yourself months to build up your business.

Drawing the Line Between
Personal Cash and Business Cash

Don't get in the bad habit of spending your own money to fund your business. Although you usually need to invest your own money to get the business started, view this as equity, not a loan. If you need to loan the business money before it becomes self-sufficient, pay yourself back with interest. The same goes for loans from friends and family. Your business was created to give you money, not the other way around. The next time your business comes begging for money, keep your personal purse zipped and figure out a way for the business to make its own cash. By making these rules for yourself up front, you'll be less likely to fall into the sympathetic lender trap.

> ### Chic Caution
>
> DON'T SPEND THE BUSINESS'S MONEY LIKE IT'S FREE. YOU WANT TO MAXIMIZE ANY TAX WRITE-OFFS YOU GET FROM LEGITIMATE BUSINESS EXPENSES. BUT REMEMBER, EVEN IF YOU CAN WRITE IT OFF, IT IS STILL AN EXPENSE, SO DON'T LIVE IT UP ON THE BUSINESS TAB IF YOU CAN'T YET AFFORD TO.

When you first start your business, you must determine how much of your own money you are will-ing to forfeit in pursuit of your business dream. This may come in the form of depleting your savings, selling off all or part of a stock portfolio, liquidating your 401(k), taking equity out of your home, running up your credit cards, or pledging personal guarantees; the answer will differ according to such things as your age, dependents, and financial goals. People also vary in the weight they put on the future versus the present, and all investments are about forgoing something in the present for an anticipated better future. Choose what is right for you, but realize these are important choices to make and consciously decide what you are willing to risk. Then, do all you can to get a return on your investment and turn this into a great decision.

While money is important, it is also important that you *never* fall in love with the money to the exclusion of anything else. Chic Entrepreneurs are not in love with money; they are in love with the dream of turning their ideas into value, which will then precipitate money. That said, money is critical to your ability to make your business work. Whether you are a startup, a ten-year-old company, or a hundred-year-old company, how much cash you have on hand—and can access through financing—will dictate the speed at which you can move, progress, grow, change, and do all the things

Chic Tip

FACTORING COMPANIES WILL BUY YOUR RECEIVABLES AND ADVANCE YOU EIGHTY TO NINETY PERCENT OF THE CASH BEFORE YOUR INVOICE GETS PAID. THEY CAN HELP YOU FLOAT CUSTOMERS WHOSE THIRTY- TO NINETY-DAY TERMS MIGHT OTHERWISE CHOKE YOU. LANDING THAT BIG-FISH CLIENT OFTEN MEANS TAKING WHATEVER PAYMENT TERMS THEY GIVE YOU BECAUSE THEY HAVE THE CLOUT TO DICTATE THE TERMS. BEFORE YOU WALK AWAY FROM THAT BIG DEAL WITH WAL-MART BECAUSE YOU CAN'T FLOAT YOUR OPERATING EXPENSES FOR THREE MONTHS UNTIL PAYMENTS START TO COME IN, SEEK OUT A REPUTABLE FACTORING PROFESSIONAL (IN THE SEA OF LOAN SHARKS THEY OFTEN INHABIT) AND CONSIDER THE TYPES OF CREATIVE FINANCING OPTIONS THAT THEY CAN PROVIDE. MAKE SURE YOUR NET PROFIT MARGIN EXCEEDS THE PERCENTAGE YOU ARE PAYING (USUALLY AROUND THREE PERCENT).

that you want to do with the business. Money is simply gas; it gets you where you want to go. If you are interested in making rapid progress toward your business goals, you must master the art of attracting money.

Forecast the Future and Buy Accordingly

Inventory management is another key element of cash management. If you go out and spend all of your cash on a product that sits in your store or a warehouse waiting for customers to buy it, all of your money is tied up, leaving you strapped and unable to do other things like advertise, hire more people, and pay your bills.

There is a balance between having cash in the bank and being able to fill orders quickly for good customer service and efficiently for smooth operations; you must find that balance. You do that by running numbers and, quite frankly, by taking a good guess. How many sweaters do you think you can you sell next month? Measure your previous sales and...guess again. Once you get good at guessing your expected sales, you can start to call it by its formal business name, a sales forecast; but no matter what you call it, don't ever forget that it is really nothing more than an educated guess. As things get more complex, your entire supply chain becomes a multi-layered educated guess. You need to continuously tweak your inventory-management model, as you forecast future demand levels and adjust inventory levels accordingly, while always being

> ### Chic Tip
>
> LEARN TO READ AND UNDERSTAND YOUR FINANCIAL STATEMENTS. COMPARE YOUR ACTUAL EXPENDITURES AND REVENUES FOR EACH MONTH WITH WHAT YOU PROJECTED AND ADJUST ACCORDINGLY.

careful not to let your ego get in the way of an intelligent sales forecast.

In addition to sales forecasts, your business-owner arsenal must include accurate and timely financial statements. If you are not comfortable in the accounting role, it is okay to outsource to an expert in this area (but not okay to outsource to any schlub off the street who demonstrates a moderate grasp of addition and subtraction). But even if you add a trusted accountant or wiz bookkeeper to your team, realize that you still need to know and understand the numbers. You can outsource the work, but not the responsibility. Make consistent financial reports a part of your business and use them as a management tool. You are the one who is ultimately responsible for your business finances and for using knowledge of the numbers to drive the business forward.

Don't Blame the Money; It Is Only a Tool

I've had many entrepreneurs tell me, "If I just had some more cash, I know I could make this business work," or "All we need is just one big sale, and then things will really start to take off," or my favorite, "If we could only find an investor to give us some money, that would fix all of our problems." Cash-flow management can be one of the most stressful parts of managing a small, growing company, draining both your time and energy. However, bear in mind that money is not the only, or even the most important, tool that you have at your disposal. Do not view money as a savior; in fact, having lots of cash can induce people to make bad business decisions. So, whether you have a lot or a little, be sure to give good thought to how you are managing your cash.

> ### Chic Tip
>
> FIND COMPANIES THAT LINK ENTREPRENEURS WITH INVESTORS (VENTURE CATALYSTS AND PEER-TO-PEER LENDERS) BOTH IN THE NEAREST MAJOR CITY AND ON THE INTERNET. THEY CAN GIVE YOU GUIDANCE ON YOUR BUSINESS PLAN AND INVESTOR PITCH AND WILL GIVE YOU THE OPPORTUNITY TO PRESENT TO VENTURE CAPITALISTS AND ANGEL INVESTORS. REMEMBER, THOUGH, THESE PEOPLE ARE LOOKING FOR A BUSINESS WITH SOME MAJOR LEGS AND A LOT OF INHERENT VALUE ALREADY BUILT INTO IT. YOU NEED TO BE DOING WELL WITH YOUR MODEL BEFORE YOU TALK TO OUTSIDE INVESTORS.

While you may not know when money is coming in, you can control when it goes out. Bad cash flow is not a business problem; it is merely a symptom of a real problem. If you are strapped for cash, look internally to seek out what you could do within the business to remedy the management problem behind the symptom. Where are your calculations off? Are you charging high enough prices? Are you maximizing productivity? Are you factoring in every fixed and variable cost? The devil is in the details. Whether you're detail-oriented or not, you need to understand the numbers and how they relate to each other.

Put a Leash on Your Burn Rate and Control Your Costs

Cash-flow management is also a character test, and one that you must master early on, because market readiness is a key component to the success of your company. Banks will tell you that character is one of the five Cs of credit[4], so make sure yours is

---

[4] Capacity, capital, collateral, and conditions are the other four.

strong. When the market is ready, willing, and able to accept your value proposition, cash comes into your business freely; before that point, however, you can burn through a lot of money if you are not careful. You must spend your cash wisely so that you can stay afloat during the lean times and be prepared when the market is ready for you. Unfortunately, no one knows when the market is going to be ready. So until that time, you must keep your burn rate (the rate at which you are spending your cash) as low as you can. The longer you can conserve cash, the longer you can wait for the

> ### Chic Tip
>
> PAY YOURSELF THE LEAST AMOUNT YOU CAN FOR AS LONG AS POSSIBLE. WHEN YOU HAVE A JOB, THE GOAL IS TO MAXIMIZE YOUR SALARY; WHEN YOU HAVE A BUSINESS, YOUR GOAL IS TO MAXIMIZE THE VALUE OF THE BUSINESS. WHEN YOU DECIDE THAT YOU ARE GOING TO TREAT YOUR BUSINESS AS A BUSINESS AND NOT AS A JOB, YOU MAKE A POWERFUL SHIFT IN MINDSET THAT WILL ENABLE YOU TO PUT THE BUSINESS FIRST IN ALL OF YOUR BUSINESS DECISIONS. STAYING TRUE TO THIS MOTIVE WILL HELP YOU TO PRIORITIZE WHERE YOUR CASH IS BEST SPENT.

marketing timing to be right. Demonstrate your willingness and commitment to repaying any debt that you might have by making regular, timely payments to build a trustworthy track record.

In order to conserve your cash, you must control your costs. No matter how much of your product or service you provide, your fixed costs do not change. An example of a fixed cost is your rent. No matter if five or five thousand people come into your shop or restaurant, you will still pay the same amount in rent. Your variable costs, on the other hand, will rise and fall depending on your production level. Therefore, if you

> ### Chic Caution
>
> ESTABLISH YOUR BUSINESS CREDIT, BUT DON'T PUT YOUR HAND OUT TOO SOON. THE LONGER YOU CAN WAIT, THE CHEAPER OUTSIDE MONEY WILL BE. LENDERS WILL GIVE YOU A BETTER INTEREST RATE AND INVESTORS WILL DEMAND LESS OF A STAKE IF YOU CAN SHOW A RECORD OF PROGRESS AND ACCOMPLISHMENT.

serve five thousand meals, your variable costs will be higher than if you sell five.

I've met business owners who assume that if you buy a steak for five dollars and sell it for ten, you make a profit. This seems like it would be true, until you factor in your other costs (e.g., the gas and labor it took to prepare and serve the steak and the cost to launder the linens and wash the dishes). If your fixed costs are high, analyze them in terms of activities to find ways to cut them. What is the cost of every activity you must perform to take your raw materials and resources and turn them into a finished product/service? To determine this, identify each activity in your process and the length of time it takes. Allocate a proportionate share of the fixed costs to each activity. Then, you can see where your most expensive portion of the process is. When many different items share overhead, you can also use such activity-based costing to dissect profit margin per product or service line. This will help you understand what products or services are most profitable so that you can make business decisions accordingly. The more you understand your financials, the better equipped you will be to run and build a successful Chic Empire.

It is important to know your break-even point, whether you are launching your business or simply a new product. Always be aware of what it takes to break even (including both fixed and variable costs) and know how to do cost-benefit analysis on new projects.

Weighing costs and benefits and making a business decision are the essence of being the strategic leader of the company.

Meet Wanda and Willie

Wanda and Willie are two small business owners with very different views on cash-flow management.

Wanda's business, Catering Connection, handles parties ranging from ten to two hundred. A true food lover, Wanda began her business by catering for her friends and family during summers and holidays, when she had time off from her job as a teacher. Wanda knew how to pick the perfect dishes for her clients, and she prided herself on satisfying her customers and serving food in bulk that tasted like it had been carefully prepared for one.

When Wanda began spending more time on her menus than her lesson plans, she decided to quit teaching and cater full time. During her first year in business, Wanda networked all over town. She made sure to expense out her meals and the cost of networking events. She met and worked with several wealthy

> ### Chic Tip
> TAKE ADVANTAGE OF POINT PROGRAMS ON THINGS THAT YOU FREQUENTLY PURCHASE, LIKE BOOKS, OFFICE SUPPLIES, FLIGHTS, HOTELS, OR RENTAL CARS. GET A BUSINESS CREDIT CARD THAT LETS YOU EARN REWARD POINTS OR CASH BACK.

clients and put on lavish events, sure she was making enough to show handsome profits.

Wanda was having fun depositing those big checks in the bank. She wasn't ever any good at math, but she could tell she was making a lot of money. She didn't take the time to crunch the numbers or to do future projections; she figured as long as she had enough money to pay her bills, things were good. Knowing that finances weren't her strong suit, she decided to do what she had always done: hire someone to do the math for her. Her accountant always did her taxes at the end of the year, so she didn't see why this year would be any different. Wanda dutifully kept her receipts, and filed everything in ascending date order in a shoebox next to her desk. She was proud of her organizational skills.

After Wanda's accountant finished her taxes, he presented her with bills totaling over $10,000 payable to the federal and state governments. A few days later, she received premium notices for the insurance on her catering van and her business liability policy that came to over $2,000. Wanda logged onto her banking account, and saw that she definitely did not have enough to cover these bills. She shuddered at the thought of her dwindling savings and was perplexed by this turn of events.

Wanda's accountant took fifteen minutes to explain to her that this is why she should have paid estimated taxes during the year. All the money she took in needed to be taxed, and this big bill was the price she paid for waiting until the end of the year to deal with it. If she didn't know what she was spending, how much she was making, or what her cost structure was, this type of problem was inevitable. He told her she should invest in some accounting software and hire a bookkeeper to do her books at least every two weeks. He gave her the names of some bookkeepers he knew and recommended she prepare for the next fiscal year by creating an annual budget and setting up a tax-planning meeting with him so that they could explore strategies for minimizing her tax burden and determine her estimated quarterly payments. He said this meeting would take about an hour and he would charge her his normal billing rate. Clearly, he understood how his business model worked.

Wanda had been so busy cooking and networking, she didn't take the time to get on top of her business expenses, or produce and analyze her financial statements. With these looming bills, she knew she'd never be able to afford that Delta flight to see her sister in Texas over the summer. She'd have to keep an eye out for a special from Southwest.

Now meet Willie. Willie owns a landscaping business, The Green Mile. He started in his spare time with a borrowed truck, one lawnmower, and a leaf blower, while working as a garbage man for the city.

Willie began his business to make extra money. However, he had always been a hard worker, and he liked the autonomy and money his business provided, along with the gratification from his satisfied customers, which is why he decided to quit his job and make landscaping his career. Before he took that leap of faith, however, Willie decided to run it by one of his customers, an accountant who ran a company that provided small businesses with a part-time Chief Financial Officer (CFO). Willie showed him what he had invoiced and spent during his first five months in business, and the CFO-for-hire ran the numbers and told Willie that he would have to charge higher prices, buy more equipment, and hire three employees before he would be able to clear sustainable profits.

> ### Chic Tip
> HIRE AN ACCOUNTANT WHO WILL DO MORE THAN JUST ADD UP YOUR NUMBERS FOR YOU. FIND SOMEONE WHO CAN GIVE ADVICE, AS WELL. MEET WITH THEM PROACTIVELY TO PLAN THE YEAR AND USE THEM AS A SOUNDING BOARD FOR BUSINESS DECISIONS.

Willie wasn't deterred. He kept working for the city and over the next six months, bought the equipment he needed, and started charging higher prices for his landscaping services. In the beginning, this angered his longstanding customers, but when Willie told them about the conversation he had with his CFO and his desire to own a successful business that could uphold his commitment to high-quality service, almost everyone understood and agreed to the higher rates.

Willie meticulously kept track of his overhead and labor costs, refined his sales and expense projections, and continued to seek advice from his CFO about his growth and other investments. Soon, Willie could afford Microsoft Office Accounting Professional, which he used to stay on top of his bills, account balances, and spending. Now, just two years later, he owns three company trucks, six lawnmowers of different sizes and capabilities, four leaf blowers, three hedgers, and a myriad of other lawn-manicuring tools. Willie also employs six full-time and two part-time employees, and has never missed a payroll.

What Can We Learn From Wanda and Willie?

The only real reason businesses go out of business is that they run out of cash. So keep close tabs on your coffers. Whether you are just setting up your business or reassessing your cash position, take all the time you need to stay on top of your financials. This is a part of business that many women hate, which could explain why women-owned businesses yield much lower profits than those owned by men. Learn to love managing your money. Get good at it and hire people you can trust to help you. Chic Entrepreneurs have a handle on their finances. They charge a fair price for their products and services based on well-thought out financials, and they enjoy counting the money as it rolls in.

How Chic are You?

DO YOU HAVE A SEPARATE BUSINESS BANK ACCOUNT? DOES IT HAVE MORE MONEY IN IT THAN YOUR PERSONAL ACCOUNT OR LESS? YOUR BUSINESS SHOULD HAVE A BIGGER BUDGET THAN YOU DO.

🔺 Are you keeping a ledger in your car to track your business miles? Keep a notebook in your car and date each page. Write down where you went, whom you met, and the beginning and ending mileage for every trip. You'll need to know total business miles and total personal miles for your taxes, so if you drive a lot for your business, get into this habit.

🔺 Do you have a petty-cash account that you use for business expenses? Be sure that you track and record all expenses, whether or not they come with a credit card receipt. Record cash expenses on a petty-cash voucher form. If you have a lot of cash business expenses, designate a separate pocket in your wallet for business cash, to make sure it doesn't get mixed up with personal cash.

🔺 Do you bank online? Online banking is great for the convenience factor, but remember the importance of building a good relationship with a business banker.

🔺 Have you met with small-business loan officers at your bank, just to get to know them? Such people can be of great value, as they are well connected in your local business community. Turn them into a fan of your business.

🔺 Are you often surprised by your bank balance? While you may not know the numbers exactly, you can have a reasonable feel for how much money you've got at any point in time, as well as what's going out and what is coming in.

🔺 Have you ever missed the date for a payment and had to pay a late fee? If so, I hope you vowed never to let it happen again. Get your bills organized and paid on time, every time. If you can't do it, get someone who can. Doing

ANYTHING LESS IS JUST PLAIN STUPID. YOUR CREDIT IS AN IMPORTANT ASSET WORTH PROTECTING.

👠 DID YOU FINANCE YOUR EQUIPMENT WITH YOUR CREDIT CARD AND BUY YOUR INVENTORY WITH THE PROCEEDS OF A TEN-YEAR LOAN? MATCH WHAT YOU BUY WITH THE TYPE OF FINANCING THAT MAKES SENSE FOR IT. INVEST IN CAPITAL ASSETS WITH LONG-TERM MONEY, LIKE A LOAN, AND USE SHORT-TERM FINANCING LIKE A CREDIT CARD TO FINANCE EXPENSES AND INVESTMENTS WITH A MORE IMMEDIATE PAYBACK HORIZON.

Chapter Six

Generic or Nike:
Sales and Marketing Go Hand in Hand

I'll admit that I'm no stranger to generic brands. During my startup days, I certainly had times when pinching pennies was necessary, and going generic can be an easy way to maximize a limited budget. I've grabbed the NO-AD Sunscreen on the way to the beach and bought the generic tomato soup for one of my mom's semi-homemade recipes, but there is an undeniable tradeoff that takes place when you choose the no-name product over the branded one. When quality matters, consumers, including myself, are generally willing to pay a little (and sometimes a lot) more to purchase their favorite brands. This is evidenced by the fact that brands like Campbell's and Neutrogena are going strong even though their products are on the shelf right next to their generic clones. Are the products inside the packaging really that different? Sometimes it is arguable, but brand names give a perception of quality and a promise of consistency. With a brand name comes the certainty that you are getting a superior product or service, as well as a sense of identity: Brands can make us feel like we are the person we want to be. You might buy generic acetaminophen for yourself, but for your newborn baby, nothing less than Baby Tylenol will do. Why? Because it makes you feel like a responsible mom. It's quite amazing, really, how much people will pay for feelings. Generic will do in a pinch, or when we're strapped for cash, but buyers' feelings often drive them to pay a bit more for what they perceive to be "the good stuff."

Nike is a fine example of a company that has excelled in the area of branding. The company started with one man's idea that there was a market for athletic shoes designed by athletes, so he began selling custom-made shoes out of the trunk of his car at track meets. As sales grew, he adopted the succinct brand name Nike, after the Greek goddess of victory. Flash forward nearly thirty-five years, and Nike is a worldwide household name.

Since the company's inception, Nike has done a fabulous job tying the brand to its iconic logo. The swoosh is now synonymous with Nike when standing alone, which is the ultimate goal for a logo. The Nike brand promises not just quality, but an experience. That didn't come by accident. Over the years, Nike has worked tirelessly to position itself in a crowded market, and after achieving sizeable market share in athletic shoes, expanded into other athletic gear. The company has used many forms of marketing, including print and television advertising, celebrity spokespeople, billboards, and sponsorships, to obtain the dominant position in the athletic-apparel industry. As consumers' tastes and behaviors have evolved, Nike has refined its image to keep it relevant. The company has not always done the right thing and had to overcome negative publicity and activist groups when news of affiliated Asian sweatshops got out. Despite the challenges, however, Nike has retained the top position and has come to symbolize not just quality, but also a healthy, fitness-oriented lifestyle and the ability to overcome obstacles, along with personal mastery, a release from daily stresses, and, of course, victory. Nike's brand, commercials, and products have turned perspiration into inspiration, and inspiration sells.

People around the world aspire to have the Nike experience. They buy the brand because they want to recreate the feelings Nike's marketing instills. As a Chic Entrepreneur, you want to create a brand that inspires your customers in the same way. Whether it's to have the cleanest toilet on the block or to run the Boston Marathon, people want to be inspired by the brands they buy. They want to feel better for having purchased them. Such intangible elements of the purchase experience are just as, if not more, important than the tangible ones. Brand creation and perpetuation come from marketing and sales working together. Let's look at how you can become a Nike.

What Is Marketing, Really?

Many startup business owners think that they can't afford to do marketing. This is usually because they mistake marketing for advertising, but marketing encompasses far more than commercials, billboards, and magazine ads. Marketing is really everything your company does to get and keep customers. It is how people view your company, from the first impression to the last, and everything your customers experience in between. Everything you say, do, and create has to have the same consistent image, because it is your face to the marketplace. Marketing is not optional; you do it whether you mean to or not, and you just might do it poorly if you don't put the proper thought into it. Marketing can also be like fashion, in that we all think we have a good sense of fashion. Nobody thinks that they dress unattractively, yet when you look around, it is clear that some people do. So don't rely solely on your own opinion of your marketing, because you might look like the emperor in his new clothes. Get a second opinion (or more) from an impartial observer—not someone you are paying.

Chic Entrepreneurs know the importance of looking good, as well as the importance of having a strategy for getting their messages out to their target markets. People like to buy beautiful things, so everything about your product, packaging, and marketing materials needs to be attractive. Marketing includes the way you answer the phone and the way a product or service looks in a store or on the web and extends to the business name and everywhere it is printed, so pay attention to all of these details in order to create a successful brand and prepare customers for the sale.

> ## Chic Tip
>
> USE THE POWER OF PICTURES TO MAKE YOUR MESSAGE REALLY COME ALIVE. USE GOOGLE TO FIND FREE IMAGES THAT YOU CAN LEGALLY USE. THERE ARE ALSO WEBSITES WHERE YOU CAN BUY PICTURES AND USE THEM ROYALTY FREE. IF YOU FIND THE PERFECT IMAGE TO DRIVE YOUR MESSAGE HOME, IT MIGHT BE WORTH INVESTING A FEW BUCKS IN IT.

Crafting Your Marketing Message

You've got your product or service and a business name. Now what? You need to build a brand; and to do that, you need a marketing message to tell people what you do and why they should care. When it comes to marketing, less is more. Being able to sum up the purpose of the company in five words or less is much more valuable than a five-page brochure. Buyers operate in glances. They glance at a book and decide if they like the title. Next, they glance at the back jacket to see if they like the content. Then they glance at the first page and decide if they like the author's voice. What does your business look like at a glance?

Think of marketing and sales as a grand seduction. The purpose of marketing is to create interest and draw customers in, but you can't seduce everybody with the same message. First, you must choose the object of your seduction so that you can consider your audience in everything you do. Next, contemplate what you want them to think about you. Do you want them to regard your company as hip or conservative, fast-paced or stable, innovative or experienced, forward thinking or traditional? Pick out words that you want people to ascribe to your business and make sure that every aspect of your marketing and your customer experience proves them to be characteristic of your company. Marketing must have credibility to count. You cannot build a company on hype alone. You must be authentic, trustworthy, and an expert at what you do. Your marketing message needs to link what you can do with what people want. Once you know who you are, and what your market wants, you can start to build your brand.

Building a brand means standing for something in the mind of the consumer. What do you stand for? Your brand personifies your company. However, if the actual customer experience differs from the brand image, that experience will trump your brand image. This is what many people miss about branding: Consistency is the key. You want to develop a brand promise and keep it. From your corporate identity (logo, business cards, stationery, signage, website) to the customer experience, it all must promise and deliver the same thing. You cannot tell the market one thing and then behave differently, because the purpose of brand is to develop trust. Your brand must be true to the vision of what your company really is, in addition to what, how, and why you sell. Brands have the power to cause people to choose one product over another, to pay more, and to stay loyal in the face of new competitors; they do not have the ability to convince someone to repeatedly purchase a product that does not live up to the brand promise.

The Easiest Way to Get People to Buy
Is to Sell Them What They Want

We talked about creating something of unique value. Now you need to tell your target market something that is worth talking about. Why do people buy? The textbook answer is that customers buy for benefits, but in the real world, customers buy for all kinds of reasons. You must figure out what your target customers' reasons are and tailor your marketing and sales strategy accordingly.

It is much easier to sell people what they want than to sell them something they do not already desire. Your product might be new,

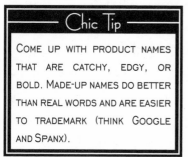

Chic Tip

COME UP WITH PRODUCT NAMES THAT ARE CATCHY, EDGY, OR BOLD. MADE-UP NAMES DO BETTER THAN REAL WORDS AND ARE EASIER TO TRADEMARK (THINK GOOGLE AND SPANX).

but you can link it to a pre-existing desire. What is the primal desire that your product/service satisfies in your target market? Does your market want skinnier thighs or whiter teeth? Do people want to feel sexy, smart, or indulgent or do they want others to see them as healthy, socially responsible, or trendy? People want to be happy, feel safe, have fun, and enjoy sensory pleasures. They want to be free from pain and problems. They want to feel attractive and successful. They want to be liked by other people and to like and feel good about themselves. What are the benefits of what you sell? Your benefits should be central to your marketing message. Remember, people buy for emotional reasons, but they like to justify those emotional motivations with a logical story to make themselves seem practical. Therefore, your marketing message needs to have both sides.

Should You Advertise?

Starbucks created a powerful brand with no advertising[5]. The same is true of Google[6]. Each company created a new and/or better experience that got people talking. Unlike most large corporations, which you would not look to for guidance on marketing, these two took a more grassroots approach. By being subversive, they became ubiquitous. As a general rule, when it comes to marketing, don't try to play with the big boys. You'll never beat them at their own game, so find another game to play instead. Big companies with multimillion-dollar marketing budgets don't have to be compelling. Their ads just give an impression, reiterate their branding, and remind people of their company. For instance, when you see a creatively colored swoosh, you immediately think of Nike and remember that you need new running shoes.

Since your company is not yet a household name, reinforcing your branding will not do. Instead, you need to follow the AIDA approach to marketing by creating Attention, Interest, Desire, and Action, in that order. Avoid traditional mass-market advertising, as it is often ineffective and cost prohibitive. Instead of just getting your name out there, you need to grab your targets' attention by cutting through the clutter of all the other marketing that bombards them. You do this by showing that you are different. Next, pique their interest. Give them a taste of what you can do for them. Cite your results. Make them wonder how you do that and create a desire within them. Make them understand the gap between their current state and the future state you are promising. Make them think, *I would be better off if I had that.* Finally, call them

[5]Starbucks turned to traditional advertising for the first time during the 2007 holiday season, to re-energize the brand by launching a national television advertising campaign, after store visits dropped for the first time in company history.

[6] Ironically, Google, the Internet advertising king, shuns traditional advertising and continues to rely largely on word of mouth and media attention. The company spent $188 million on advertising and promotion in 2006, about one-sixth of what Microsoft spends, and according to some, is the most valuable brand on the planet.

to act. Tell them what you want them to do next. The action you prompt does not have to be a purchase; you could ask them to send away for a free booklet or CD, check your website for promotions, or sign up for your newsletter. Ideally, you want them to opt in to receive communications from you. This is what we call getting them in "the sales funnel." Fill the fat end of the funnel with many prospects early in your sales process, narrow this pool of leads by qualifying who are mere suspects and who are actual good prospects, and put them through a sales process that will cause some of them to eventually trickle out of the end of the funnel as customers. Marketing and prospecting techniques like cold calling, direct mailers, or ads that tease people with free offers and ask them to opt in to communications with you are excellent ways to fill your funnel. Once people agree to let you talk to them, you can stay in front of them, so that when they do have a need for what you do, you are the one they think of first. Your challenge is to become known.

> **— Chic Tip —**
>
> CREATE A COLLAGE OF YOUR TARGET MARKET BY LOOKING THROUGH MAGAZINES FOR PICTURES OF PEOPLE WHO ILLUSTRATE YOUR TARGET CUSTOMERS. CUT OUT THESE PICTURES AND GLUE THEM TO A POSTER BOARD THAT SAYS "OUR CUSTOMERS" ON THE TOP. HANG THE COLLAGE IN YOUR OFFICE TO REMIND YOU WHOM YOUR COMMUNICATIONS ARE ADDRESSING.

When I flip through a magazine or see commercials flash by, I may or may not remember the name of the makeup company paying for the spot, but when a girlfriend tells me that I simply must try the new Kiss 'Em Krazy lipstick, I most likely will. People like to pass along things they think others will enjoy. Whether they are recommending a doctor or a YouTube video, people are constantly exchanging information on products, services, and experiences. This kind of word-of-mouth advertising is free, and it is the best way to spread your marketing message. So, how do you get it? Think about what kinds of messages are passed along: jokes, gossip, and things that are shocking, unexpected, or revolutionary. People pass along information they think others would enjoy or benefit from, so figure out how to make your message into an interesting, informative story. Another way to increase your word-of-mouth is to ask for it. Your satisfied customers will tell other people about you, but you can get them to do it more often when you tell them you want it. You also need to get word-of-mouth support from the influencers of your market. Influencers are people who are perceived as knowledgeable authorities and have a lot of interaction with your desired customers; consequently, they have pull with your target market. If you are a business consultant, you could look to attorneys and accountants as influencers; obviously, their clients trust them and would take their advice, and the best part is that almost every business has one of each. If you are selling dog food, your influencers would be veterinarians, groomers, and breeders. Who are the trusted authorities in your industry? Once you identify your market's influencers, you can begin strategically meeting and developing relationships with them. Start by telling them about the compelling value you provide to the market. Once you have demonstrated that you are credible and trustworthy, ask them to keep you in mind and spread the word about your business. You can even increase their enthusiasm about your company by giving them a branded gift, a free sample, or a referral incentive. You only get what you ask for, so ask for word-of-mouth marketing.

There are several other ways to get the word out without paying for it. Send periodic newsletters to your friends and family, former and current customers, networking acquaintances, and everyone you meet. You can also host an informational seminar, panel, or roundtable on a topic of importance to your target audience, which will allow you to reach a network of contacts and affiliate channels and educate people about your unique offering. It will also serve as a tool for positioning yourself as an expert in your field.

Utilize the Media

Public relations is a powerful way to tell the world about your business. Launching a PR campaign includes ongoing activities to ensure that your company has a strong public image. Even if you can't yet afford to pay a public relations think tank to get your name all over the newspapers and airwaves, you can still use the media to

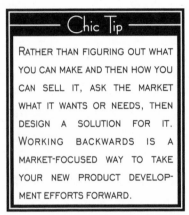

create a buzz about your business. No one is going to knock on your door with a reporter and camera crew though, so take the initiative and start getting in front of the local media. You're not going to end up on *The Today Show* tomorrow, but some savvy networking could get you in the local news. The media is constantly seeking news. That's their job.

Chic Tip

RATHER THAN FIGURING OUT WHAT YOU CAN MAKE AND THEN HOW YOU CAN SELL IT, ASK THE MARKET WHAT IT WANTS OR NEEDS, THEN DESIGN A SOLUTION FOR IT. WORKING BACKWARDS IS A MARKET-FOCUSED WAY TO TAKE YOUR NEW PRODUCT DEVELOPMENT EFFORTS FORWARD.

Thus, meeting and cultivating relationships with the right people and having something interesting to say when you do can make you a local celebrity. At the very least, it will get you known by the media so they are already primed when your business has bigger and better news in the future.

In order to pitch yourself in the right way, you have to learn how the media think. Watch the TV shows you think you could be on and read the publications that you think might feature you to see what kinds of stories they like. Stay abreast of current events and look for an interesting angle you could use to make your small business their big news story. Most magazines have what's called an editorial calendar, where they plan out what each month's focus will be.

Determine how you can fit in with one of these themes and pitch them an idea well in advance. Also, find out when publications are involved in events, such as awards luncheons, quarterly dinners, charitable activities, or forums, so you can rub elbows with their journalists.

When you talk to or meet with the media, make sure that you have real news to deliver. This is when you use your succinct marketing message and brand image to impress them with your uniqueness. Depending on what kind of business you have, what you do might be compelling enough, or perhaps there is a human-interest story behind the work. What is special about your employees or customers, or one in particular? Did one of your customers use your product or service to propose to a girlfriend, save their family from starvation, keep their home from collapsing, or bring their pet safely back home? What is the weirdest thing that has happened at your office or the wildest story you have heard from a customer? People like to read about people.

Your compelling message could also be about how you operate:

- Do you use green practices?
- Do you use robots or unusual technology?
- Is your office in an odd location?
- Do you donate to charity or volunteer?
- Do you use all organics?
- Have you an interesting holiday or seasonal tradition?

To get your story in front of the media, you'll either want to send a press release or call and pitch it to someone. Use the right tool for what you want to accomplish. As with all of your marketing efforts, it is important to understand your objective before you start using random tactics to try to achieve it. For instance, posting your press releases on PR websites can help with search engine optimization (SEO) and drive traffic to your website, but is not likely to get people to your store's grand opening. If your story has a great visual element to it, or you otherwise think it is a better fit for TV, call or email the appropriate editors rather than writing a full press release. Introduce yourself briefly and professionally, and succinctly describe your story and your angle. If they think it would be interesting to their audience, they just might take it. Pitching a story can also work for getting timely news into print. If you feel that you have a knack for coming up with good headlines and would like to get your business in print, buy a how-to book on writing press releases and creating media lists. Remember that even though technically "free," these tasks take time and your time is valuable. As a business owner, you must constantly ask yourself where your time is best spent.

Execute Your Marketing Strategy

Once you've created a brand and a message that speaks to your target market, it's time to execute a cohesive marketing strategy. Below is an example of how your marketing plan might look, complete with a suggested timetable. Include a RESULTS column where you can record the effectiveness of each tactic.

TACTIC	WHEN	HOW	WHY	RESULT
Press Release	Monthly	Send to targeted media list and post to PR websites	To develop media relations, get free mentions by neutral 3rd parties	• Call from Weekly Times reporter • Quoted in article • Employee Smith mentioned in New Hires section of Gazette
Host an information seminar, panel, or roundtable	Quarterly	Advertise to a network of contacts and affiliate channels	To cultivate the image of an expert	• Strengthened partnership with XYZ • Grew email list by 50 names

TACTIC	WHEN	HOW	WHY	RESULT
Newsletter	Every other month	Email newsletter with valuable content to prospects, network contacts, current customers, friends, family, etc.	Consistently keep your brand in front of those in your funnel	· Two referrals to new clients · Grew email list by 35 names · Positive comments from friends · Introduction to a new influencer
Chamber of Commerce	Twice a month	Network with complementary business owners and service providers to develop strategic alliances	Increase visibility of the business and increase referrals	· Met three potential partners · Met two potential outsourcing partners · Got two new customers · Asked to sit on the board next year

Once you have laid out your marketing plan, assign all activities necessary to execute each tactic among everyone who has a role in the execution so you can be certain each task is performed by the dates required to keep the plan on track. Since each tactic might require several small steps, put together a project plan and post all relevant dates in an online calendar (optimally one that is shared by you and your employees), with automatic reminders set up to give you enough lead time to get each piece ready and out on time. I know how easy it is to lose track of time as an entrepreneur. A pre-set schedule of marketing events is the best way to make sure you are executing your plan.

Marketing Leads the Horse to Water
and Sales Makes it Drink

> ### Chic Tip
>
> TRY OUT THIS PHRASE: "I RECOMMEND THAT YOU. .". IF YOU FEEL HESITANT ABOUT PUSHING YOUR PRODUCT ON SOMEONE, TRY THINKING OF SALES AS RECOMMENDING A COURSE OF ACTION. AS AN EXPERT IN YOUR FIELD, AND A CARING ONE AT THAT, YOU ARE SIMPLY DOING OTHERS A SERVICE BY IMPARTING YOUR ADVICE. BY PUTTING YOUR FOCUS ON SHOWING PEOPLE THAT YOU GENUINELY CARE ABOUT THEM AND HAVE THEIR BEST INTERESTS AT HEART, RATHER THAN CLOSING THE DEAL, YOU'LL ACT WITH INTEGRITY AND BECOME A TRUSTED ADVISOR, INSTEAD OF APPEARING DESPERATE, SELFISH, OR UNSCRUPULOUS.

Once you look good, sound compelling, and execute consistently, people will start to notice you, at which point, you'll need a sales process to turn prospects into customers. Different businesses require different levels of direct sales. Whether you are selling directly to individual customers, larger clients, or distribution outlets, or writing a sales pitch for your website, sales skills are an essential part of your job as an entrepreneur, and it will serve you well to develop them. I have met business owners who say they don't want to do sales and would prefer to hire someone else for that role, but it is imperative that entrepreneurs be the sales champions of their companies. You know your business better than anyone else does, so if you can't sell it well, no one else will be able to. Besides, if you are like most small companies, you can't afford to pay someone to sell your product at the beginning. If you've never been in sales before, fear not. The sales process, just like cash flow, can be learned.

Think of the sales process as if it were a theatrical play. For your sales play, you must take the time to script out all the parts, including all possible responses you could get in opposition. No matter what your audience's response is, be completely prepared. All responses can be anticipated, even the negative ones. After you write your script, you'll be able to execute the sales process as if you were acting out a play. People respond in kind as you create the flow. If you can get your prospects talking, they will usually tell you what it will take to sell them. By understanding the true problem, or what they are really looking for, you'll know whether or not your business has the right answer for them. Once you determine what they want and why, you are in a good position to close the deal.

Chic Tip

USE PHRASES LIKE "TELL ME MORE ABOUT THAT" TO OPEN THE CONVERSATION UP, AND CLOSED QUESTIONS LIKE "WHEN WOULD YOU LIKE TO GET STARTED?" TO PIN PEOPLE DOWN TO A DEFINITIVE ANSWER.

Dig for more information, uncover buying motives, and instill urgency by asking prospects questions such as:

- What seems to be the problem?
- What caused that to happen?
- How long have you been looking for a solution?
- How does that make you feel?
- What have you tried?
- And how did that work?
- Why do you think that didn't work?
- How much longer can you afford to keep going like this/to wait?
- What will happen if you do nothing?
- What are you planning to do about this problem now?
- What would your ideal solution look like?
- At what point would this be considered a crisis/urgent?

When asking these questions, make sure to focus on the person. Many people try to sell by using industry jargon that explains the process of their product or service, but this can be a turnoff to a customer. Remember, they are not experts in what you do, and your product constitutes only a small portion of their lives. Don't make them become an expert; guide them with your expertise. Speak to your customers in their words and talk to them about

Chic Tip

GET COMFORTABLE WITH SALES BY FINDING A SALES GURU WHOSE STYLE FITS WITH YOUR PERSONALITY. LISTEN TO SALES TAPES IN YOUR CAR, ESPECIALLY WHEN YOU ARE ON YOUR WAY TO A SALES CALL. BEFORE YOU GROAN, LET ME TELL YOU THAT SALES TAPES ARE FUN TO LISTEN TO; YOU WILL LOVE HOW EXCITED THEY MAKE YOU. REMEMBER, EVEN IF YOU AREN'T SELLING YOUR PRODUCT OR SERVICES, YOU ARE ALWAYS SELLING YOURSELF. SO MAKE SURE YOU ARE GOOD AT IT. KNOWING THE WORDS TO A TOP-40 SONG WON'T HELP YOU IN YOUR PRESENTATION TO A PROSPECT, SO SWITCH TO SOME EDUCATIONAL AND MOTIVATIONAL CONTENT INSTEAD AND GET PSYCHED TO SELL.

results, not the process you take to get there. They're not buying the how; they're buying the what. Don't sell your customers a reverse osmosis water filtration pump; sell them clean drinking water for the better health of their families. Realize you're not selling a new hair product; you're selling admiring looks from strangers all day long.

Once you have scripted the ideal scenario, cast it with your ideal prospects, those who have the interest in and means to purchase your solution. Now, bring these people through "the sales funnel" we talked about earlier. Engage them in the sales process by identifying their particular needs and addressing those needs with the benefits that your solution provides. Once you understand how long your typical sales process takes, you can calculate how many deals you can expect to close based on your current pipeline of prospects. You can also estimate how many prospects you need in order to reach your revenue goals. With a well-honed process, sales simply become a big numbers game instead of a series of scary hit-or-miss events.

Make Your Sales Process Easy

If you asked someone out on a date, and they told you that

you'd have to pick them up in a remote, hard-to-find, bad neighborhood, and that they lived on the fifth story in a building with a broken elevator and no nearby parking, at what point would you say, "You know what, maybe we should just meet somewhere," or just back out of the date entirely? In essence, that is what many businesses do when they are courting customers. No wonder no one wants to start a relationship with them. Sales are all about building relationships with people, which starts by building

> **Chic Tip**
>
> PUMP UP YOUR SELF-ESTEEM. IN ORDER FOR OTHERS TO HAVE CONFIDENCE IN YOU, YOU MUST EXUDE CONFIDENCE IN YOURSELF. THE BEST WAY TO SHOW OTHERS THAT YOU FEEL GOOD ABOUT YOURSELF IS TO SMILE. WHEN THE SALES JITTERS GET TO YOU, LET THOSE PEARLY WHITES DO THE TALKING.

rapport from when you say "Hello." Getting customers is like flirting and keeping them is like marriage, only you are allowed to have as many customers as you can attract, without any pesky polygamy charges getting in the way. Bat your eyelashes with some good-looking marketing collateral, get to know them by asking them to tell you more about themselves, take them out on a few fun dates by giving them a taste of what you do and the value that you provide, and what it would be like to have you as a partner. Make them want to consummate the relationship, ask for their commitment, and seal the deal.

> **Chic Tip**
>
> PEOPLE COMMUNICATE BEST THROUGH STORIES, NOT LISTS OF FACTS. MASTER THE ART OF TELLING A GREAT STORY THAT YOUR PROSPECT CAN RELATE TO ABOUT SOMEONE WHO EXPERIENCED A CHALLENGE SIMILAR TO WHAT THE PROSPECT IS GOING THROUGH AND HOW YOUR COMPANY HELPED.

All things being equal, people buy from people they like, and when all things are not equal, they still buy from people they like. The way to increase your likeability is to increase your self-esteem, like yourself, and like what you do.

Genuinely believe in and effectively communicate the value that you bring to others through what you are selling.

Get a Final Answer

Good communication is essential to developing good customer relationships. Just like all plays, yours requires dialogue. Remember, you have two ears and one mouth—use them in that proportion. Listen to your customers. If they trust you and believe that you can help them solve their problems, they will usually tell you everything you want to know. After questioning prospects, it is your turn to present. Before you tell them how great things could be with your solution, twist the knife a bit by painting a picture that makes them really feel the pain of their current situation. Finally, show them how your solution would alleviate this pain.

> ### Chic Tip
>
> FORCE CLOSURE. WHEN YOU SUBMIT A PROPOSAL, ALWAYS GIVE AN EXPIRATION DATE ON YOUR OFFER. IT IS PERFECTLY REASONABLE AND MORE PROFESSIONAL NOT TO KEEP AN OFFER ON THE TABLE INDEFINITELY. THIS WILL HELP TO CREATE A SENSE OF URGENCY BY SHOWING BUYERS THEY HAVE A LIMITED WINDOW OF OPPORTUNITY. BY INSTILLING A SENSE OF URGENCY, YOU ARE ACTUALLY DOING PEOPLE A SERVICE, BY FORCING THEM TO COME TO A DECISION.

There are only two good answers in sales: yes or no, and you need to be okay with either. Often, people will avoid the tough questions or let customers give them a maybe response in order to avoid the dreaded "No." This is a waste of time. *Maybes* will kill you as an entrepreneur. It is better to ask the tough questions and get the real answer to your sales pitch than wait for the sales process to drag on.

Get Your Customers Involved
in Your Market Research

Don't conduct your marketing and sales efforts in isolation. Instead, look for ways to involve customers. Time spent getting to know your market is rarely wasted. Some of the most successful products and services on the market today were designed using intimate customer contact. Observing customers in their natural state, interviewing them, having them complete surveys, and holding focus groups could yield great data to help you design better products and learn the best way to sell to and serve your desired customers. Feasibility testing is a smart way to increase your odds of making the idea-to-business leap. Once you have some initial sales, continue to talk to and learn more about your customers to create a profitable and sustainable line. Have a goal for what percentage of your customers you expect repeat sales from and a strategy for how to make that happen.

Competitive Analysis and Market Position

It is better to choose your competition than to have it chosen for you, so it is critical that you be proactive and pick your rivals as part of your strategic positioning. You can rapidly move closer to a mainstream market when you define your competition and position your product within a buying category that already has established credibility or visibility with your target buyers. Thus, by carefully positioning your company, you can piggyback off the market demand your competitors have created with their advertising influence.

Chic Entrepreneurs play nice and never bash the competition. They are cunning enough to get around them without getting their hands dirty. When someone asks about your competition during a sales conversation, your answer can be, "Oh yes, I'm glad you asked about them. Would you like to know our points of difference?" Responding in this way gives you the opportunity to differentiate on your terms. Since people will usually answer a question of "Would you like to know...?" with a "Yes." Then, you'll get an opportunity to sell them on your unique value. Remember, your points of difference need not be why you are better, because you don't even have to be better; you just have to be a better fit for the customer. Don't fear a reference to your competitors; it is often a gift. Hearing about them from customers and prospects allows you to keep tabs on them, and gives you guidance on how you can convince your ideal customer that you are the right fit for them.

Keep in mind that the difference doesn't even have to be tangible. Think about why people buy Coke over Pepsi. Some would say it is for the taste, but I would argue that it has a lot more to do with the brand, even if customers don't consciously realize it. Most people don't even admit their real buying motives to themselves, let alone to others, because as I mentioned before, buying motives have a strong emotional component, yet people like to think of themselves as logical. Thus, your point of difference need only be a perception with a logical framework behind it. If you hit the chord properly based on what you've learned about them, most of your prospects will only need a little nudge to see why you are the obvious right answer for them.

Picture This...

Since most people are visual, include some kind of visual element in your presentation, even if it is just the use of visual language like:

- Imagine enjoying...
- Picture yourself...
- Others will look at you with envy.

- I can see you in something like this.
- This one looks like you.

This is especially important if you have nothing physical for them to touch, feel, or try on. You can make your prospects start to feel like customers by picturing a new reality in which your product or service is now theirs. If they like the way that new reality feels, they'll let you keep talking. Visual language is a powerful way to mix some show with your tell and keep your customer engaged in the shopping experience.

Talking About Price

Once you've got someone interested, there comes a time to start talking money. Your price determination should come by assessing perception of value, not by evaluating costs or marketplace conditions. Make it your goal to find your maximum price point; only a rookie entrepreneur would charge less than what she could. Get comfortable with your price. Before you start discussing your fees (or your new hike in fees) with anyone, you need to get comfortable with them yourself. There is nothing to be ashamed of when commanding fees that are equal to the value that you provide. People can always hire a lesser business. The confidence you show when you talk about your price

Chic Caution

AVOID THE USE OF BLAND WORDS. MAKE THINGS MORE INTERESTING BY USING MORE LIVELY LANGUAGE. REPLACE *LEARN* WITH *DISCOVER*, AND *NICE* AND *GREAT*, WITH *STUNNING* AND *SUPERB*. GET RID OF *STUFF* AND OTHER NON-DESCRIPT VAGARIES AND ELIMINATE FILLERS SUCH AS *LIKE* AND *UHM*. INSTEAD, BE MORE SPECIFIC OR BE SILENT UNTIL A CLEAR THOUGHT COMES TO YOU.

IN ORDER TO HELP TRAIN YOURSELF AND EVEN YOUR STAFF TO REFRAIN FROM USING THESE WORDS, CONSIDER USING A JAR THAT YOU PUT AN IOU FOR FIFTY CENTS IN EACH TIME YOU USE THE WORD DURING THE WORKDAY. AT THE END OF THE YEAR, CALCULATE THE IOUs IN THE JAR AND DONATE THAT AMOUNT TO CHARITY. YOU'LL SOUND MUCH MORE PROFESSIONAL—AND TRÈS CHIC!

is priceless. Additionally, when talking about the price of your product or service, speak in the language of investment, rather than fees, prices, or costs. No one likes to pay fees, everybody thinks prices are too high, and people are always looking for ways to cut costs, but everyone likes to make a smart investment. So, refer to your asking price as just that—an investment. By phrasing it this way, your customers will focus on what they are getting in return, not what they are giving. If applicable, you can even develop an ROI model in an Excel spreadsheet that shows the return on their investment when they input their own numbers.

Money is not the number one decision-making factor for customers, no matter what people tell you. People buy for many reasons other than price, just like people date for many reasons other than looks. For many, price doesn't even matter. In fact, for the customers you really want—the ones who truly want your unique product or service—price is a mere detail. If you offer to solve people's problems in exchange for something less valuable to them, they will take the deal. So, create a "deal" with benefits that far exceed the outlays and they won't be able to refuse.

Ask for Their Business

Asking for the sale itself is an often-overlooked step in the sales process, yet it is a necessary one that will greatly increase your close rate. In the sales conversation, you will want to help your potential customers think through all of their "what ifs." Once you have done that, it is your duty to ask them to move forward, and you are doing them a disservice if you do not ask. Thus, begin the objections, since it is quite natural for people to throw up an objection after getting an offer. Do not panic, blurt out the first thing that comes to mind, belittle them, or lie. Objections are really just a prospect's way of asking for more information. Through them, the prospect is giving you directions on how to close the deal. Be sure to listen to the objection carefully, put a thoughtful expression on your face, and nod to show empathy. Ask for clarification to make sure you understand the objection, and then briefly and clearly explain why this particular point is insignificant or how you can turn it to their advantage.

Once you have your yes, proceed. Don't lose your poise, or show any sign of relief or surprise. Smile confidently as if you knew all along that they would make this smart decision. Tell your prospects how much they will enjoy your product and confirm that they have made the right decision. Provide them with what you promised you would, and follow up with customers after the sale to confirm that you met or exceeded their expectations. Your purpose of follow-up is to ensure satisfaction, and thus positive word-of-mouth, as well as to ask for referrals and/or identify cross-sell opportunities.

After each sales encounter, it is also important to conduct a win-loss analysis to understand and document why some meetings are successful, what tactics didn't work, what you were pleased with, what you wish to repeat, and what you'd like to do better next time. To create a winning culture in your organization, you must celebrate your successes. Develop your own ritual for celebrating sales within your company. I have seen them vary from ringing a bell, to banging a gong, to sounding a horn, to sending out an email blast or a mass voicemail. Develop your own ritual that you do each time you announce a new win. Include a celebration, a communication, and recognition for the key players

---

Chic Tip

TIE A PORTION OF ALL NON-SALES EMPLOYEES' COMPENSATION TO SALES AS WELL, SO THAT WHEN YOU WIN, THEY WIN. DON'T WORRY IF YOU CAN'T AFFORD TO GIVE A LOT. THE AMOUNT IS LESS IMPORTANT THAN THE GESTURE ITSELF. UNLIKE WITH COMMISSIONED SALES PEOPLE, SMALL INCENTIVES MOTIVATE SALARIED EMPLOYEES JUST AS MUCH AS BIG ONES.

involved. Celebrating victories is part of what makes work fun, as it should be, so go have some: You got a sale!

Finding Salespeople

As you expand, you might need more feet on the street, at which time you'll need to find salespeople. Start looking for them before you need them. Until you are a mature business with good margins and a proven process, you can't afford to pay for someone's learning curve, so experience is a must. There are plenty of industries that recruit young, attractive go-getters right out of college for sales jobs. Large companies put these new employees through a comprehensive sales-training program and send them out to knock on doors and cold call. The high rejection rates are grueling, particularly in a pure commission-based environment, and result in a high degree of turnover, leaving these recruits ripe for the picking. They have gotten good training and are relatively young, which means cheap, and are thus ideal candidates for small businesses. Always remember, though, that everyone within the company can do sales and marketing. Do not confine these vital activities only to those who have one of these words in their titles. Ultimately, sales is not a function of one department; all of your employees can be salespeople of sorts, even if they are just selling their friends and families on the great place they work.

Finally, be sure to measure your results. Whether your marketing efforts center on print ads, web marketing, networking, or all of these and more, you need to measure the effectiveness of these techniques and the ROI on the resources you've committed. Every resource, especially time, has value, so hold each resource accountable for generating the highest possible return.

Meet Adrienne and Alisha

To make these principles really come alive, let's take a look at how Adrienne and Alisha executed on sales and marketing in their small businesses.

Adrienne opened a boutique clothing store, Adrienne's, in an upscale shopping district with many other independently owned stores. As she researched where to locate her business, Adrienne noticed that even though this area had other boutiques, none of them were fashion boutiques. She also noticed that people who lived in the surrounding neighborhoods fit her target demographic: young, wealthy, urban trendsetters. Adrienne concluded this would be the ideal place to set up the boutique of her dreams.

Adrienne had enough money to pay rent and utilities for six months, buy inventory, place ads in the city's free weekly newspaper, and keep some cash in reserve. She bought a grand opening sign for the front of her store and paid her landlord to order a sign with her store's name. Unfortunately, however, when the sign came in, the scripted style Adrienne requested made the name look more like Adrime's. *Whoops.*

Adrienne told all of her friends and family who lived nearby about her store and ordered T-shirts made with "Yo Adrienne—Open Up" printed on them. She had a graphic artist design postcards advertising Adrienne's House of Fashion, with a map showing the store's location. Unfortunately, however, the map was incorrect, and the dot marking the shop was two blocks south of where it was supposed to be. *Oh well,* she thought, *they look good, and I'm sure people will be able to figure it out.*

Adrienne tried to use multiple marketing vehicles, but they lacked any kind of cohesive element. At the grand opening, Adrienne's friends and family all took one of her custom T-shirts and hung out in the store, and some local foot traffic stumbled in to have a look as well. Adrienne figured that her friends and family would be walking billboards wearing these T-shirts, and her best friend even bought an expensive pair of jeans, netting Adrienne $175 that day. She was off to a fabulous start.

The next day, after the buzz of the grand opening party had worn off, Adrienne found herself alone in her store all morning. She was very surprised when only two people happened through during the entire day. Both of them asked Adrienne how to pronounce her store's name.

In the next week, Adrienne only had twenty-five customers and only sold $750 worth of merchandise. Adrienne had been keeping store hours from 10:00 AM to 6:00 PM, like most of her neighboring stores, but she noticed that the bulk of her customers came through from 5:00 to 6:00 in the afternoon. She decided that she needed to stay open later and changed her hours from 10:00 AM to 8:00 PM, which caused her traffic to increase slightly, along with her profits. However, the longer hours started to wear on her and her perkiness as a salesperson began to wane.

After her first month in business, Adrienne barely managed to break even. Because she had banked on a profit to buy inventory for the next season, she had to tap into her personal savings to buy the merchandise she needed. In an effort to spur some sales, she decided to print up flyers with a twenty-percent-off coupon on the bottom to give to customers who came into her store.

Two months after Adrienne's grand opening, Patty, who owned the wine store around the corner, came in to browse. Patty told Adrienne that she was surprised to see another clothing store open in the area. When Adrienne asked why, Patty informed her that the mall had driven the last two clothing stores out of business. While Adrienne knew that there was a large mall nearby, she was unaware that it had caused two other fashion boutiques to close. Her landlord had told her the owner of the previous fashion store had chosen to retire, and she had assumed that foot traffic from the neighborhoods would keep her business afloat.

To increase her traffic, Adrienne called the local free newspaper and placed a half-page ad for her store offering a twenty percent discount on the total purchase. Next, she sent out a postcard to all the residents in the surrounding neighborhood that asked, "Have you visited Adrienne's?" and included pictures of some of her latest clothes and a small picture of the mall in the bottom corner with a red no sign through it. Adrienne didn't realize that when prospecting for sales, you should always ask questions that most people will answer with a yes, as opposed to a no. Nor did she realize that when you are the smaller competitor, it is unwise to directly name your competition, as it gives your better-known adversary free marketing and reminds your target market of your own shortcomings.

With all of these extra out-of-pocket expenses starting to add up, Adrienne had to tighten her own budget by switching to generic brands at the grocery store. Even worse, she could no longer afford to wear her own designs—so much for being her own best salesperson. At the end of six months, Adrienne still wasn't netting a profit. Since her marketing plan had not been completely thought out or consistently executed, and her branding lacked coherence, her sales suffered.

Now meet Alisha, and hear her story. After losing her purse once, and having it stolen one night when she was out on the town, Alisha had begun to carry her money in her bra. Of course, this wasn't the most convenient or secure practice with a regular bra, which is what made her begin thinking of creating a bra made to hold money. She knew that it was a unique idea and that women just like her would love it for travel or nights out when they didn't want to carry a purse. That was how Alisha invented The Bralet™, the bra wallet. The Bralet had a slim pocket inside the bra cup with just enough room to hold a few credit cards and a small amount of cash. Alisha designed it herself and sewed her first prototype by hand.

When Alisha decided to turn her idea into a business, she started by creating a marketing and sales plan. Jaded by traditional advertising and knowing that no one could sell The Bralet like she could, she decided to do her own marketing and public relations—with the help of a few close friends. She had a friend design a logo of the word Bralet, turning the B into a purple bra with straps. She found a bra manufacturer to produce a prototype and started calling department and travel store buyers to introduce herself and her new product with the tagline, "Keep your stash close to heart." The edgy tagline appealed to the fashion-forward crowd, and when Alisha got an appointment with a buyer from a major department store chain, she decided to do something bold. She wore The Bralet to the meeting and demonstrated how it worked by whipping her business card right out of her Bralet, telling the buyer that every woman would want one of these in her bra collection. A month later, The Bralet was being sold in that department store chain. Two months later, a popular travel store chain picked it up and featured it in its catalog.

That's when Alisha began calling on her friends and family to go buy one and rave about the product in the store, to their friends, and in online blogs. Alisha also arranged to do in-store tutorials with the sales associates, because she knew that she was The Bralet and wanted to personally transfer her enthusiasm for her product to every person responsible for selling it. After she got the sales team pumped up, she stayed for hours introducing customers to The Bralet herself. She then started her own blog about The Bralet and told people to visit it to talk about their experience with the product. Alisha became notorious for pulling her business card out of her bra every time a woman walked by.

Alisha also called numerous women's magazines and TV shows to pitch her product and soon got significant media coverage for The Bralet. She even sent out product samples, along with personal notes, to several young female celebrities. When she turned on the TV and heard a late-night talk show host make fun of The Bralet in his monologue, she knew she had really created a buzz. With her brand intact and sales going strong, Alisha set a goal to get an appointment with Nike within a month to pitch an athletic version of The Bralet.

Adrienne vs. Alisha

Adrienne failed because she lacked a cohesive marketing strategy. The inconsistency of her brand, both visually and in name, left no lasting impression on her target customers. Adrienne wasted money by giving away free merchandise to people who were already loyal to her, mistakenly thinking a T-shirt would be a motivational sales vehicle, and placing ads in publications where her return on investment was uncertain. Although she felt like she did her research, she had in fact overlooked the most important thing: her predecessors. The fact that similar stores had not fared well in this neighborhood was vital information that she missed and could have acquired easily had she chatted with the neighboring shopkeepers before signing her lease. Adrienne falsely believed that sinking money into advertising would do all of her marketing for her, so she didn't capture important customer information. Her failure to do sufficient market research on her location put her in defensive mode, which ran counter to the premium niche she was trying to occupy. Rather than finding a way to create more perceived value, Adrienne began discounting her merchandise, which had the exact opposite effect.

Alisha, on the other hand, is as chic as it gets. She is not only a hard worker, but is also a smart worker, especially concerning her marketing and sales strategy. Instead of looking for someone to pass the buck to, she took full ownership of marketing and sales and delivered. She trademarked her name, came up with one consistent message and made everything in her company speak that message. She had a logo designed and stuck to that look. She found influencers for her target market and got them to mention her product. She got her friends and family involved, specifically asking that they support her by actively doing something. She held her cool during crucial sales meetings and demonstrated her own flare by simply being herself. She turned intrigue into interest by demonstrating the product to everyone. She recognized the need to go beyond being a good salesperson to create a great sales force and made it her job to teach those in touch with her prospects how to sell her product. She created a way to get feedback from and keep in touch with her customer base, thus making them identify even more with her brand. She recognized the importance of future product development and once she achieved success, she strategically built on it by leveraging her existing marketing efforts and brand name.

How Chic are You?

⬆ DO YOU LOOK LIKE SOMEONE FROM WHOM YOU WOULD BUY YOUR PRODUCT OR SERVICE? NO ONE WANTS TO BUY CLOTHES FROM SOMEONE WHO LOOKS GRUNGY (UNLESS THE CLOTHES ARE GRUNGE) OR LEARN THE SECRET TO SUCCESS FROM A SHAGGY DOG IN NEED OF A HAIRCUT.

🔺 DO YOU HAVE ENOUGH BUSINESS ATTIRE TO GET YOU THROUGH AN ENTIRE WEEK WITHOUT REPEATS? YOU DON'T HAVE TO SPEND A FORTUNE TO LOOK PUT TOGETHER. AN OUTFIT SHOULD MATCH, BE OF THIS CENTURY, AND INCLUDE ACCESSORIES. IF YOU CAN'T AFFORD ANN TAYLOR OR BROOKS BROTHERS, TRY TARGET AND T.J. MAXX.

🔺 DO YOU (AND YOUR SALES TEAM) KNOW FIRSTHAND ABOUT THE BENEFITS THAT YOU CLAIM TO BE SELLING? YOU CAN'T SELL WHAT YOU DON'T KNOW. TALK IS CHEAP. LIVE YOUR BRAND PROMISE EVERY DAY.

🔺 DO PEOPLE SOUND HAPPY TO HEAR FROM YOU WHEN YOU PHONE? DO THEY RETURN YOUR CALLS? IF NOT, YOU MAY NEED TO POLISH YOUR PITCH TO MAKE IT MORE COMPELLING. MARKETING WILL MAKE YOU SHINE FROM AFAR, SALES WILL GET YOU DATES, AND A CONSISTENT MARKETING STRATEGY WILL CREATE LONG-TERM RELATIONSHIPS.

🔺 DO YOU GET NERVOUS WHEN YOU START TO TALK ABOUT THE PRICES OF YOUR SERVICES? STRENGTHEN YOUR BELIEF THAT YOU ARE WORTH IT BY WRITING YOUR HIGHEST PRICE, FOLLOWED BY THE WORDS, "IS A BARGAIN CONSIDERING THE VALUE" ON A POST-IT NOTE AND STICK IT TO YOUR BATHROOM MIRROR. ADD A BIG SMILEY FACE TO THE NOTE TO REMIND YOURSELF TO SMILE EVERY TIME YOU THINK OF YOUR PRICE.

🔺 DO YOU KEEP HEARING THE SAME REASON WHY PEOPLE ARE NOT BUYING? FIX IT, ANSWER IT, OR OVERCOME IT.

🔺 DO YOU PERPETUALLY DROP YOUR PRICES IN AN ACT OF DESPERATION? STOP SHOWING YOUR PANTIES AND INSTEAD FIGURE OUT A WAY TO GIVE THE FOLKS A BETTER SHOW WITH YOUR CLOTHES ON.

🔺 DO YOU HAVE ANY MARKETING COLLATERAL? SHOW PEOPLE THAT YOU HAVE GIVEN AS MUCH THOUGHT TO YOUR BUSINESS AS YOU ARE ASKING THEM TO.

🔺 DO YOU HAVE TOO MUCH MARKETING COLLATERAL? DROWNING PEOPLE IN PAPER IS NOT A SALES STRATEGY—NOT TO MENTION WHAT YOU'RE DOING TO THE ENVIRONMENT.

🔺 DO YOU HAVE A PROFESSIONAL WEBSITE TO WHICH YOU ARE PROUD TO DIRECT PEOPLE? THE VALUE OF AN ABOUT US PAGE IS GREATLY DIMINISHED WHEN YOU'VE MISSPELLED THE NAME OF YOUR ALMA MATER.

🔺 DO YOUR BUSINESS CARDS LOOK LIKE THEY CAME OFF THE PRESS OF A PROFESSIONAL PRINTER, OR ARE THEY MORE OF THE HOME-JOB VARIETY? PEOPLE WILL SEE YOUR CARD AS A REFLECTION OF YOU AND YOUR BUSINESS.

🔺 ARE YOU STILL ON YOUR FIRST BOX OF BUSINESS CARDS? MAKE IT YOUR GOAL TO GIVE OUT AT LEAST TWENTY-FIVE BUSINESS CARDS A MONTH TO NEW PEOPLE THAT YOU MEET. SOME OF THE BEST NETWORKERS I KNOW DO THIS IN A WEEK.

CHAPTER SEVEN

Crash Dieting or Weight Watchers:
The Importance of Systematic Processes

How many times have you tried a crash diet and literally crashed? I know I have. After eating nothing but grapefruit or drinking a calorie-less concoction made of wheat grass and lemon juice for a week, I've either scrapped the diet and eaten a cake or nearly passed out in a meeting. Besides the obvious health risks, the problem with crash dieting is that it's a short-term, quick fix. Although the results can allow you to fit into your skinny jeans for one or two days, the system is not made to last. The battle of the bulge is back in no time. Worse still, repeated crash dieting will make it more and more difficult to replicate the results each time you do it. Thus, crash dieting is not the way to achieve predictable lasting results.

Weight Watchers, on the other hand, is a diet that provides a healthy, effective, and easy system to take and keep weight off over the long term. You get a set amount of points depending on your weight and are allowed to eat whatever you want (often in tiny portions), as long as you stay within your allotted points—you can even eat all the pickles you want at zero points! Many people choose to go to meetings every week, use Internet weight-loss tools, and do confidential weigh-ins at a Weight Watchers site. Others choose to count points and weigh in on their own or with a group. In addition to a systematic way to measure your food intake, you also have a systematic way to stay emotionally committed. It's a safe and easily understandable diet that does not restrict you from eating your normal foods; there are snacks that curb your hunger and desserts to satisfy your sweet tooth. While Weight Watchers may not give you the lightning-fast results that you think you need, it also won't put you in danger of downing an entire quart of ice cream in a fit of rebellion or fainting in the street. When it comes to dieting, most health experts agree that finding an easy and repeatable process for consistently managing your weight is the best way to keep it at your ideal level.

As a Chic Entrepreneur, you need to implement systematic processes that will allow you to maintain healthy business operations and keep you from crashing and burning. If your marketing strategy works, you will generate demand. You will have hit the right people with the right value proposition, and then you will have to provide what you marketed and sold to them with a dependable fulfillment process each and every time they want it. Once you know your business strategy is a good one, you must implement all aspects of that strategy through repeatable processes.

Processes allow you to create consistency. As a Chic Entrepreneur, you and your employees must develop a systematic way of doing things, instead of reinventing the wheel each time you start a new project or get a new client. These processes will enable you to perform consistently and provide a reliable customer experience. Customers want to know they can count on getting the same dependable product and service every time they come to you. Consistency builds trust, and trust breeds loyalty.

In business, your first sale is rarely the one upon which you can retire. It is with the repetition of sales over time that you create true wealth. Everything within your business can be systematized, from product development to sales and marketing, to customer follow-up, to cash-flow management. Systems and processes are how the disparate pieces of your business machine link together to create an entity of salable value that hums with or without you there. Many of my clients have been entrepreneurs who initially had no employees and therefore wore all of the proverbial hats. The need to systematize was not readily apparent because they knew everything and did everything. Consequently, they tended to treat each new customer interaction individually, never putting processes in place to systematize transactions and the role of business owner. However, having a business that is all up in the head of one or two people will eventually come back to bite you, especially if your goal is to grow. Even though figuring out how to systematize your processes can take many extra hours of work on the front end, it will ultimately save you time, money, and stress, and help you build a reputation of reliability that will make your clients comfortable recommending you to others. Tinkering with your processes to find the best way of doing things is an ongoing pursuit. Getting things to run like clockwork requires some tinkering, but eventually this accomplishment will set you free and is the difference between being a small business and owning a small business.

Whether you have a buttoned-up culture or a more casual, laid-back work atmosphere, formalizing processes shows that you are a professional. Customers expect businesses to have processes; that is one reason they are coming to you. They want to feel like you have done this before and have a systematic method that you are following. So don't disappoint. Systems will save you time and labor costs. Additionally, if you are considering selling your business at some point, the investment in good systems and processes will pay off then as well.

Use the following questions to help you come up with a few small things you can do to systematize your processes:

- Can you create customer intake forms, order forms, and fax forms?
- Do you have a frequently asked questions bank?
- Do you have templates for correspondence like form letters and standard emails?
- Do you have a server through which your employees can share files and software?
- Can you, your employees, and your customers use a document-management system to access, collaborate on, and share documents instead of trading emails all day long?
- Do you hold a weekly meeting with your employees? Do you have an agenda and have minutes taken?
- Do you do regular status checks on long-term internal projects?
- Do you provide clients with monthly or quarterly progress reports?

Flex Your Flexibility Muscle

One of your main advantages as a small business is that you're able to make changes faster because it's just you and maybe a few employees to start. If you come up with a new process idea, you can implement it today, measure how it goes, and either ditch it or make the change permanent, just like that. Big companies have to go through a plethora of meetings and decision levels to make any changes, but you can turn on a dime. As soon as you see something isn't working, start finding ways to change it, and when you observe something that is working, use it as a model for other areas and look for ways to tighten the process and make it even better.

When you first start building a business, processes form haphazardly on an as-needed basis. Processes develop over time in a fledgling business, but they don't always develop optimally. Processes and systems typically have a volume threshold, and once they exceed it, they start to bend, weaken, and sometimes break. A system or process that works well when you have two employees and thirty-five customers often becomes less efficient when you run three hundred customers through it, with a staff of twenty-five. All you want when you start your business is for it to grow, but when it does, be prepared to be unprepared for it and wise enough to recognize when your processes need to be revamped. The evolution and obsolescence of processes look something like this:

> At first, you keep copies of all of your customers' order forms, so you start filing them. As customers become repeat customers, some start having automatic billing through their credit cards; for those customers, you start a separate locked cabinet where you keep their credit card numbers and authorization forms. You hire a sales rep to focus on business accounts, and the sales rep starts filing his sales notes in another filing system, using the business name. But your secretary files things using the name of the contact person. Soon, one drawer has grown into an entire wall of filing cabinets, and

when a customer calls with a question, it takes twenty minutes to find the right file.

Or like this:

You use the inventory-management component of your accounting package to keep track of product and sales in your store. When you decide to sell online, you buy a shopping cart for your website that emails you an invoice that you need to manually enter into your accounting system. You attempt to integrate the two, but the accounting system keeps adding sales tax on every order, so you must manually override it on all out-of-state orders. For two or three sales a month, this is no big deal, but after you get featured on Fab Style TV, your web sales will soar and you will be up till two in the morning messing with the accounting system—and hoping you won't make a mistake in your sleepy state.

Chic Caution

BEWARE OF CUTTING UNTIL IT HURTS. AS YOU LOOK FOR WAYS TO IMPROVE YOUR BOTTOM LINE, DON'T LET THE QUEST FOR EFFICIENCY ERODE EFFECTIVENESS. THIS IS A DELICATE BALANCING ACT AND YOU MUST BE VERY CAREFUL NEVER TO CUT COSTS AND TIME SO MUCH THAT YOU ACTUALLY END UP CUTTING INTO THE VALUE OF WHAT YOU ARE PROVIDING.

These are the types of process hiccups you could encounter on the road to becoming a Chic Entrepreneur, and your decisions on how to design a new process and implement a new system can make the difference between experiencing growing pains and growing an ulcer. Having set processes in place gives your business stability and sets a foundation for being able to scale. Processes enable your business to create the same success over and over again. Once you've done something right, replicate, tweak, and repeat.

To know how well your business is using processes, ask yourself, "Does my business keep running well when I'm not here?" or "Does my business run well when a key employee is not there?" Businesses need not be dependent on specific people, and when good processes are in place, they are not. Develop your processes as if you were putting yourself out of a job—and your other employees, too. I am not suggesting that you look for ways to lay people off. In a growing business, there is always more work to do, so you are not literally putting anyone out of a job, but you are trying to eliminate as much work as possible by making your business more efficient, so that you can move yourself and your people to higher-value work.

The whole point of being a Chic Entrepreneur is to own a business that runs by itself so that you can do what you are best at. The point is not to learn how to do everything and run around like a chicken with your head cut off. There is nothing chic about chickens. There is, however, plenty of chic in letting yourself shine. Maybe you are great at networking or inventing products, or developing and motivating people, or building long-term relationships with clients. If you can put good processes in place, you can go to as many networking events as you want or tinker with product creation and your business will run and generate money without you getting tangled up in the middle of it.

Admittedly, you are the engine of your business in the beginning, but as you progress out of the startup stage, the business needs to have a self-sustaining source of power. It can't always be dependent on one person for everything. If that's the case, there's no way the business is generating enough money to do much more than break even, or perhaps clear a small profit. And since Chic Entrepreneurs create successful businesses, this is just not going to be good enough.

Systematizing everything within a small business starts with emptying the CEO's brain contents out onto paper—the how-to's, the expert knowledge, and the less tangible intuition, or inner genius, of the owner. All of that needs to become a process of some type, if possible. As you continue to build the company, do the same thing for every activity, deliverable, function, and department. A few years back, there was a lot of hype about so-called *knowledge management systems* that were going to allow companies to retain as much of their employees' intellectual capital as possible. Although the systems never lived up to the expectations, the concept is still valid. You need to manage the knowledge of your organization so that when someone (including you) walks out the door, the whole business doesn't fall apart.

Most business owners understand their business model on an intuitive level, but not necessarily on a process level. The first step is documentation: Map out the process flow of how things work today, breaking out all the activities that take place or need to take place in your business. This will allow you to examine your business model in action and understand how all the activities relate to each other.

Process Maps

A process map, also known as a flow chart, is a visual representation of the progression of activities within an operation. It includes starting and ending points, inputs, outputs, and decision making, together with all of the parties involved. Process maps allow you to look at everything you are doing in your business as if you were standing at the counter in a Subway restaurant watching someone build a sandwich. They allow you to see who does what, with what, and in what order. You don't need some fancy software program to create one. Just draw it out with a pencil on a large sheet of paper (a roll of brown paper works great) using circles, squares, stars, arrows, or anything else that will help you visually depict your processes. Also, be sure to indicate when an action is required and when decisions are made.

Process maps strip your business down to its bare operational bones. When you start drawing your process map, it becomes plain to see why your current way of doing an activity is less than ideal. Even more important, you will see where and how your processes can be improved. Looking at a process in a visual way makes it easier to understand the flow, the customer-facing interactions, the internal and external handoffs, and the sticking points. You can also identify the sub-processes and sub-activities that are constraining your business or your personal performance.

Mapping out everything you do also makes it easier to train new people and cross-train your existing workforce. Process mapping enables your people to see the big picture of what is going on in the company, as well as who is responsible for what activities. In order for work to flow smoothly, everybody in the organization needs to understand how their work fits in with the other pieces of the process, what the result should be, and what happens if the process breaks. Just telling someone to do one process or function, like answering the phone or creating spreadsheets, without showing them exactly how it interrelates with the rest of the business practically guarantees that you will have some problems down the line. Full comprehension will empower your employees to do their parts to the best of their abilities. It will also hold them mentally accountable for their jobs, when they know their work feeds into someone else's.

When employees understand how their work affects their colleagues' jobs, they take more personal responsibility for doing their pieces well. Benefits you can expect from sharing process maps with your employees include increased quality, teamwork, and smoother interdepartmental hand-offs, not to mention suggestions for improvements from those in the trenches. People who actually perform the process are sometimes better able to suggest improvements than those managing or overseeing the process, so let your employees know that continuous process improvement is a strategic priority and their input is appreciated. When they come to you, listen to their suggestions; your employees can be your internal operations consultants if you teach them how to be.

> ### Chic Tip
>
> BACK UP YOUR DATA. SET UP AN AUTOMATIC BACKUP TO RUN NIGHTLY OR WEEKLY. MAKE SURE YOU REVIEW YOUR BACKUP PROCESS AND TEST THAT IT IS WORKING. COMPUTERS FAIL; DON'T LET THEM CAUSE YOUR BUSINESS TO. KEEP YOUR FILES OFFSITE OR IN A FIREPROOF SAFE TO PROTECT THEM FROM FIRES AND FLOODS.

Process maps also allow you to step back and view the entire flow from the outside, without being swept up in it. This is what consultants do. Learn how to do this yourself or, better yet, condition your people to think this way, and it will be very easy to continuously improve and optimize the way you do things inside your business.

You can process map any area that you want to run more smoothly, from your front office to your back office, to your entire supply chain, which encompasses the total progression of raw materials, to work in progress, to finished goods, as well as all the planning, forecasting, and handoffs along the way. You have both an internal and an external supply chain, both of which offer opportunities to create more efficient processes, as materials pass from one party to another. Using process mapping can help you see both supply chains more clearly and increase your understanding of your external supply chain.

The first time you do any activity inside your business, you generally do not do it in the best way possible; the goal is just to get the work accomplished. However, by paying careful attention to your processes, you can optimize your organization's efficiency and effectiveness.

Here Is an Example of How to Create a Process Map

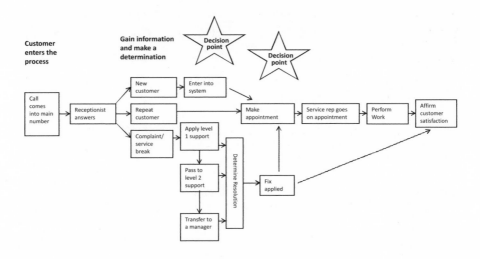

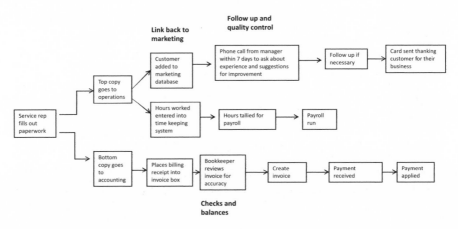

Now it's your turn. Take one process within your company and map it. Start with an easy one, like responding to a new customer order and progress to a more complex one like resolving a customer service issue.

Continuous Improvements

Your business can be like a tree that blossoms each year, bigger and better. Each year builds on the last, which is why process optimization and streamlining is not a one-time job. You must reinvent your own new best practices on a continuous basis. There is always something changing and there is always a better way to do things. Realize that there is no perfection in the art of designing processes. Your goal, instead, is to have an ongoing progression of continuous improvement that takes place systematically as part of the natural cycles of the business.

Everything can be a process. The more processes you have, the more value the business has. Once the systematic processes are in place, you start to create some momentum. When operations really get going, maximize what you've got. Really dig into that successful process for that product or service and optimize it. One of my former employers, McMaster-Carr, is a one-hundred-year-old industrial distribution company with a very interesting management strategy. Rather than seeking out seasoned executives who have worked in distribution for ten or twenty years, they hire top-of-their-class graduates from schools like Northwestern, University of Pennsylvania, Harvard, and Wake Forest, and put them to work as managers of all of the operational departments. These managers must not only manage, but also complete ongoing improvement or consulting projects within their departments. The managers are tasked with tracking all of the key metrics for their departments and coming up with ongoing projects to tweak processes and make them even better. Each manager stays in a particular area for about six months and subsequently moves on to manage another department. This business strategy allows the company to attract top talent by creating interesting and challenging positions and enjoy great profitability by squeezing every ounce of waste out of their processes. McMaster-Carr sells over 400,000 different products and ships ninety-eight percent of them from stock. To do this well and continue to wow customers (which they do), their processes need to be impeccable. Imagine improving your processes for a hundred years with the help of fresh top-tier talent. When I say you are never done with process improvement, I mean it. Streamlining is not just something big companies must do; it is vital to your organizational development as well. What can you do to create the kind of continuous improvement culture that McMaster-Carr inspires?

Even if you are super small now, you would be wise to consider your growth projections as you build your processes. Would the business be able to handle a hundred percent increase in volume? Obviously, you'd need more personnel, but if you had them, would the rest of the business be able to handle it, as it is built today? Don't build a huge infrastructure; build a flexible one. Can you have all of your employees trained in each aspect of your business so that they will completely understand how your business runs? This kind of knowledge sharing might take some time, but it might also help you if/when an unexpected emergency comes up that prevents an employee from doing her job.

Reliability

It is impossible to achieve optimum performance inside your business with flawed processes. Quality experts tell us ninety-four percent of breakdowns inside a business are due to process failure,

——— Chic Tip ———

DEVELOP A STANDARD NAMING SYSTEM FOR ALL ELECTRONIC DOCUMENTS FOR EASE OF SEARCH AND TO AVOID DUPLICATION. PUT AS MUCH INFO IN THE FILE NAME AS POSSIBLE WITHOUT MAKING IT A MILE LONG. FOR INSTANCE, IF YOU OWNED A LAW FIRM, YOU WOULD USE ABBREVIATED CASE NAMES FOR EACH FILE. THEN EVERY DOCUMENT IN THAT FILE WOULD USE THE ABBREVIATED CODE FOR THE CASE, SAY WHAT THE DOCUMENT IS AND END WITH THE DATE AND/OR A VOLUME NUMBER. FOR EXAMPLE:

COOKV.LONG_ANSWER_7.7.07

including processes that are faulty to begin with. Often, we mistakenly blame workers, but when something breaks down, it is usually a broken process, not an employee or equipment problem. That is why having a tool as powerful as process mapping is crucial to streamlining your operations and eliminating these potential problem areas. Design processes so they won't allow for anything less than the quality level you have committed to, and refine and solidify your processes to ensure excellence and repeatability.

Automate Your Back Office Operations

By automating your back office operations, you can remove the human component that takes up employee time and effort, which equals money to you. As your business grows, the number of necessary tasks and activities will increase. You cannot possibly manage and monitor, nor can you have expertise in, all of these activities. Moreover, doing things manually, one at a time, no longer makes sense as volumes increase.

Hiring employees will increase your productivity. The way to maximize your employees' efforts is to apply technology where possible to reduce human redundancy. Technology will also enable you to collect data on your processes that will enable you to make intelligent decisions for the future growth of the business. Technology will allow you to consolidate operations, eliminate inefficiencies and waste, and increase profitability. If you are not organized, there is no shame in admitting it. I know, because I can be terribly unorganized, which is why I have reached out to others who have this strength to help systematize my business. From operations consultants to custom software developers, to efficiency engineers, to professional organizers, there are plenty of experts in this field. If processes are not your thing, find someone to help you pinpoint exactly how to optimize each critical function of your business and put the best possible version of your business on autopilot. With processes in place, you can start making a lot more money, while working less. You will start to feel less frazzled and more in control, as your business hums along like a well-oiled machine. Sweeping your inefficient processes under the rug will trip you up later when your business starts to run.

Use Technology as a Business Enabler, Not Just for Technology's Sake.

Use technology as the powerful business tool that it can be, and automate anything that you can without diminishing the customer experience.

Here are some technology opportunities to consider:

- Can you purchase a phone system instead of using a receptionist or an administrative assistant?
- Can you automate your billing?
- Would cell phones, PDAs, or laptops allow you to close more sales more quickly or provide better service?
- What records can be stored electronically rather than physically? Would having searching capability be useful?
- Can meetings take place via conference call instead of in person?
- Can you use an email auto responder to keep in touch and market?

- Would it make sense to link disparate computer systems together so they share information seamlessly?
- How can technology be a business accelerator in your company?

You can get an estimate for these types of technology investments so that you can start to plan your future strategy. If possible, find an Information Technology (IT) outsourcing partner to play the role of Chief Information Officer (CIO) in your company. Nearly every company today needs someone like this, even if it is in the form of just a few hours a month from a consultant.

Beyond just gaining efficiencies, technology can also be used to create a competitive advantage. The value of technology for business is that it helps you be more systematic about everything on your to-do list. Superior technology can mean new levels of quality and innovation that can make your old way of doing things obsolete, or it can mean inventing entirely new markets. Technology is so pervasive these days that the interaction between people and technology is the most important driver of process excellence. Even if you are not comfortable with technology, do not let that deter you from looking into leveraging it in your business.

> ### Chic Tip
>
> LOOK AT YOUR WEB ANALYTICS TO SEE THE TRAFFIC PATTERNS THAT PEOPLE FOLLOW ON YOUR WEBSITE. YOU CAN SEE WHAT PAGES THEY SPEND THE MOST TIME ON AND WHAT PAGES THEY GO TO BEFORE THEY BUY. YOU CAN ALSO IDENTIFY ANY STICKING POINTS, LIKE A PAGE THAT MANY PEOPLE GO TO AND THEN LEAVE. USE THIS INFORMATION TO IMPROVE THE FLOW OF YOUR WEBSITE AND MAKE IT MORE EFFECTIVE IN GETTING PEOPLE TO THE INFORMATION THEY NEED AND TO YOUR DESIRED NEXT COURSE OF ACTION.

On the surface, my business advisory firm doesn't do anything technical; our value is in providing management consulting expertise, strategic guidance, and hands-on assistance to enable business growth. We started out only doing this one-to-one, but realized we could leverage the intellectual property that we were creating to reach more people, more efficiently; that's where technology came in. We now use technology to transmit our ideas to a much larger audience in a cost-effective manner through email, online newsletters, websites (and website optimization techniques), online article posting, a blog, business and social networking sites, online forums for entrepreneurs, and webcasts. We also use technology to communicate and collaborate internally and with clients, as well as for planning, measuring and fulfillment, and that is just the beginning. We are proof that technology can be used in many ways to enable a non-technical business. Once your business starts to grow, productivity becomes the name of the operations game. So, use processes and technology to create a lean, mean machine, and let it run.

Separate the People from the Processes

People lead your company, and systems run it. Build your processes out from the functions that need to be performed, and then give them to people to manage. As much as possible, your people should be performing checks and balances on your systems, not doing the process themselves. By focusing first on the objective of the process and systematizing the consistent achievement of the desired outcome, you can remove the human variable. Anyone who is trained and competent should be able to run the system that you have built. This way, once a process is in place, if something breaks, it is not an employee or a contractor who is to blame, but the system instead. You can fix the system, but you can't always fix people —you can coach them, but you can't change them. To become a Chic Entrepreneur, your goal is to be able to plug a person (the right person) into any portion of your business and have it work.

Entrepreneurs often feel like they need to know everything, but if you can let go of wanting to know how to do everything or being the expert in all areas, you'll be able to accelerate your progress. While it's great to be a well-rounded entrepreneur, it is foolish to try to be the expert on all aspects of your business.

Leverage and Scale
and How They Can Work for You

Systematic processes build scale and leverage into your business, thereby broadening its reach and increasing its value. By leveraging your systems across a growing customer base and product/service portfolio, you can work less and earn more. In the physical sense, leverage means you can create a great result using a small movement. Think about how a wrench works: You use the force of an arm pump to rotate the wrench, which in turn twists the small bolt it is gripping. Even though you are not strong enough to turn the bolt by yourself, the wrench's long handle magnifies the force you apply and generates enough pressure to accomplish your goal. With a long lever, you can exert a lot of leverage. Now that I've given you a brief physics lesson, let's talk about how this applies to your business.

In a business, leverage means you can make one small change and create a big result. For instance, you can send one email and reach one person, or you can send that same email to your whole list and reach thousands of people. Similarly, by issuing one press release to one reporter, your message could reach their entire readership, which might be tens of thousands. Along those same lines, by improving one of your employee's customer relationships skills, you could have an impact on the experience and loyalty of hundreds of customers. Once you have gotten some leverage, you can start to enjoy economies of scale and spread fixed costs over more transactions, essentially reducing your cost per unit of product or service and increasing your profit margin. Realizing economies of scale from your sales and marketing efforts will allow you to experience geometric growth (otherwise known as the hockey stick curve), instead of simple arithmetic growth. This is when things get exciting.

Use the following questions to gauge how close you are to the benefits of economies of scale:

- If you got one hundred new customers tomorrow, would your profit margin go up or down?
- Does each new customer generate more or less work?
- Do you feel as if you are always reinventing the wheel or just spinning the wheel?
- Do you still have to work just as hard in your processes as when you started, or are things getting easier each time you do them?
- Have you noticed a learning curve that once you or your employees get beyond enables you to do things a lot faster?

Systems and People Are Your Real Assets

Anything you can translate into a repeatable system becomes a business asset, just like people, equipment, inventory, and your less tangible, but all-important, brand image. We tend to appreciate the value of equipment more than intangible assets because we paid a quantifiable amount for the physical

---

Chic Tip

START BUILDING YOUR CLIENT DATABASE AS SOON AS POSSIBLE AND MAKE SURE THAT YOU COMMUNICATE WITH CLIENTS ON A CONSISTENT BASIS (E.G. E-NEWSLETTERS, EMAILS). PERSONALIZE MASS CORRESPONDENCE BY USING THE "INSERT NAME" OPTION TO GET A MESSAGE OUT TO EVERYONE QUICKLY WITHOUT LOSING THE PERSONAL TOUCH.

assets, and if you can stub your toe on it, it seems more real. Your people and processes are of great value. Moreover, your equipment is a depreciating asset, while your systems are appreciating assets, becoming more and more valuable as you improve and refine them. Systems are a big component of what someone would pay if you ever wanted to sell your business. No matter what field you are in, you must have processes to make your business hum. Processes will obviously differ radically across industries, as will the systems used to support them. How you set up and monitor them, what functions they perform, and what you keep in house versus outsource will depend on your company and its market, but good processes will always add value.

Having processes in place also gives you the confidence that will keep you from stressing out about short-term problems and helps you avoid capriciously jumping from one tactic to another in search of a quick fix that has no lasting value. When you have systematic processes in place, you know that if you lose customers, you will get more due to the marketing processes you've got in place. If someone quits, you will hire someone else who is just as good, using your hiring process, and they will ramp up quickly using your training process. If your products get dated, your product development process will create

> ## Chic Tip
>
> ONCE YOU'VE PUT PROCESSES INTO PLACE, PRACTICE TAKING YOURSELF OUT OF THE BUSINESS, TO SEE HOW IT WORKS WITHOUT YOU. DO SOMETHING FUN DURING WORK HOURS—CATCH A MATINEE, GO GOLFING OR SHOPPING (NOT GROCERY SHOPPING, REAL SHOPPING). PERIODICALLY REMOVING YOURSELF FROM THE BUSINESS WILL GIVE YOU A TASTE OF WHAT IT FEELS LIKE TO HAVE THE BUSINESS RUN ON ITS OWN AND IT WILL MOTIVATE YOU TO MAKE IT EVEN MORE SYSTEMATIC. IT WILL ALSO IMMEDIATELY HIGHLIGHT THE PARTS OF YOUR BUSINESS THAT STILL NEED BETTER PROCESSES PUT INTO PLACE. ANYTHING THAT BREAKS DOWN WHEN YOU ARE NOT THERE NEEDS A PROCESS AND PEOPLE WHO ARE TRAINED TO RUN AND MANAGE THAT PROCESS.

new ones. If your customers start to leave, your market research process will tell you why. If your competitors start to encroach on your market share, your strategic planning process will help you come up with a way to retaliate.

Customer Participation

Engage your customers in your processes. We are in the age of self-service and customers actually enjoy being involved in part of the work. Building customers and their actions into your business processes can both increase satisfaction and lower costs. Some forms of customer self-service give the customer control over the part of the process in which decisions are made; others simply have the customer do some of the manual labor. If designed well, your process can make the customer have fun taking over part of the process, instead of feeling burdened. ATMs, self-scanning grocery checkout, and make-your-own Bloody Mary bars are all examples of getting customer to do the work, under the guise of making their experience fun and/or easy. Some people have even made an entire business out of letting people do the process. Think of the places where you paint your own pottery or design your own T-shirt, and I'm sure that somebody somewhere has implemented the make-your-own pizza place conceived by *Seinfeld's* Kramer. However, you need to make sure you teach your customers how the process works and what their role is before letting them loose in your self-service processes. If you don't tell them how to do things the best way, your customers could get frustrated and produce poor quality output, and you could experience errors and subsequent rework, time delays, and system failures.

Meet Nancy and Nicole

To put this in real-world terms, let's look at two business owners, Nancy and Nicole.

Nancy owns a temp agency, Temp*tation*. Nancy had worked in human resources for ten years, so she has an extensive background in people placement. After helping three friends find better jobs, Nancy, a stay-at-home mom, figured that she should be paid for her skills. She decided to provide employers with highly skilled administrative, technical, and project-management professionals.

Nancy was not very computer proficient, so she ran a largely paper-dependent office. However, she did have her own highly developed system for organizing the business. Nancy brought candidates in, had them fill out a paper questionnaire, and take proficiency tests to show where they might be best suited. She noted their marks on the designated space on their applications and filed them, along with any other relevant work documents, alphabetically according to last name. She also kept information on each of her client companies. Her employer files included payment policies and standards, information about company culture, dress code, and all the key contacts.

In the beginning, when it was just Nancy finding companies seeking employees and job candidates looking for placement, this system worked well.

Nancy was making profits and starting to work so many hours that she decided to hire two part-time employees. Nancy explained her system to them and after a few weeks, she felt that things were running along smoothly again. Nancy's business kept growing, as more and more employers heard that the snazzily named Temptation could find them great employees fast, and soon she hired three full-time employees and moved her entire operation into new office space.

However, Nancy's business was outgrowing her system, which had worked fine for her, and reasonably well when she added her first couple of employees. Now, the filing cabinets had multiplied and it was becoming increasingly difficult to find applicants with specific experience without poring over the files for hours at a time. To compound this situation, by the time they found and called a suitable candidate, they often discovered that the person had already found another job. Since Nancy's team could usually get through a list of employees and find several to interview for a particular position, the cumbersome process was invisible to clients at first. However, over time, the strain began to show on her employees' desks, which were covered with piles of résumés.

As set in her ways as she was, Nancy could not ignore the fact that her company couldn't grow without becoming a paperless office. Every time she watched her employees sort through file after file, she had visions of stacks of dollar bills flying out the window. It was painful to watch her hard-earned money pay people who were crippled to inefficiency by the very processes she had created. After reading about the possibilities of searching for documents in an online document-storage system and the efficiency and backup safety that secure online hosting provided, she decided to start storing files on the Internet. However, getting the existing files on the new system was a slow task that took up most of the time of one of her part-time employees, without earning Nancy any revenue. Moreover, now her employees had to search both computer and paper files, which made the process twice as long.

As she kept taking on more and more clients, the complaints about how long it took Temptation to find suitable candidates began to mount. Unfortunately, since she did not have the income to hire another employee to speed things up, Nancy was forced to turn away business. Then one of her key employees, Suzy, left for another job with a larger corporation that had a fully automated system that not only enabled it to take on more and larger staffing projects, but would also permit Suzy to focus on the more interesting aspects of staffing and do less of the grunt work. This was a huge blow, since Suzy had been with Nancy the longest and knew how everything worked. Everyone had come to rely on Suzy and viewed her (over Nancy) as the one with all the answers. Nancy had never really documented what Suzy did operationally or what criteria she used to make decisions. There were many things that everyone just took for granted with Suzy around, and now no one knew the process for doing anything, from picking candidates to getting food catered for lunch meetings—or even making coffee. Nancy wasn't sure if she should hire someone new or put her business on a crash diet to slim down her staff and reduce all of the waste before starting all over again in a more organized fashion.

Now meet Nicole. Nicole grew up in the restaurant business, having worked in her family's Greek restaurant as a busgirl, server, hostess, salad chopper, and line cook, over the years. She knew all of the jobs that were needed to prepare food, get it to customers on time, and clean up afterward, but not much about the business side; her mother and father had always taken care of that.

Nicole wanted to open her own restaurant, with fare that was a fusion of Greek and American cuisine. Armed with menu ideas and her mom's secret baklava recipe, Nicole decided to learn what she didn't know about running a successful restaurant. She read some business books and took a few night business classes, one in which she wrote a business plan for a restaurant that served casual fine dining fast in the financial district of her city. Nicole had identified this need when she dated an investment banker who worked downtown. During the week they would meet for lunch, and Nicole observed that the food court in the main downtown mall always did a massive amount of business at lunchtime, as did the fast-food places in many of the large office buildings. However, when she talked to servers at nearby restaurants, they told her that foot traffic was generally slow at lunchtime and that the people who did come in only had forty-five minutes and consequently wanted to go ahead and pay for their meals immediately after ordering. Others called in large take-out orders, which could back up the kitchen and leave servers without tips, which led to a great deal of costly turnover.

Nicole decided that her mission would be to provide financial district workers "fine dining in forty-five minutes or less, guaranteed." Nicole came up with her restaurant's name, The Grecian Bank, and found a vacant warehouse that used to be a catering hall that could easily be converted into a restaurant. With her business name and her forty-five-minute promise painted in thick black letters on the restaurant sign, Nicole needed highly efficient floor and kitchen staff and an extremely well developed communication system. Therefore, she decided to invest in top-of-the-line headsets for all of her staff so they could communicate walkie-talkie style.

From her experience in her family's restaurant, Nicole knew that several small issues had the potential to cause large delays in the service process. For example, the cappuccino machine was usually very slow, so if multiple orders came in simultaneously, servers would be standing in line waiting for it, delaying their ability to serve their other tables. In some areas of the restaurant, tables and chairs might get positioned too close together and, depending on a patron's girth, servers could be forced to take long and indirect routes to get from table to table. However, the issue that Nicole believed affected service time the most was the process of entering each meal course in the computer, which sent tickets to print in the kitchen. Whenever more than ten patrons dined at the same time, terminals were in high demand. She remembered feeling impatient, tapping her foot, waiting for other servers to finish inputting their orders and thinking, *There has got to be a better way to do this.*

In one of her classes, Nicole read case studies about companies that had used technology as a competitive advantage to provide a superior experience by doing something faster, cheaper, or better. This made her start to think about augmenting the restaurant's computer system with a wireless network of devices that would allow for more efficient placement and timing of customer orders, which would result in fewer delays in service and increased customer satisfaction.

Nicole learned that many restaurants and stadiums already used handheld devices to input orders and figured out that she could place these same devices on tables with clear, short instructions for patrons, thereby eliminating the need for a large wait staff. Once seated, customers could view the menu and place their own orders. The devices would also give patrons the ability to text message a question about the menu to the floor manager and receive a response. Nicole anticipated that this system would reduce the time between when customers were seated and when their orders reached the kitchen from twelve minutes to six. Next, Nicole hired hosts and hostesses, bussers, food runners, and floor managers to seat customers, clear tables, serve food, and manage the process.

Nicole decided The Grecian Bank would serve lunch and dinner. During shifts, floor managers, dressed in all-black uniforms with nametags, would deal with service and timing issues. If a customer's order did not come out of the kitchen in ten minutes, an automatic signal would be sent from the kitchen to the floor manager's beeper showing both the table number and order number. The floor manager could then speak to the kitchen via their headset and determine what was needed to help speed up the process in the back. The floor manager could help plate the food, deliver the food to the table, or give the table an update or an appetizer. Nicole had wisely empowered floor managers with the authority to offer complimentary appetizers in such instances. Based on floor plans and speculative workload, Nicole decided that she needed five floor managers on the lunch shift and three on the dinner shift.

Nicole also decided to add a credit-card swipe onto the table devices so that people could self-service their checks. This would eliminate the wait for the server to bring the bill, which would average six minutes in a similar restaurant, and ensure that people could leave when they wanted. Patrons who wished to pay in cash were directed to press a button to page a floor manager when they were ready to pay. Since this system made tables turn over faster, the restaurant was also able to serve more patrons.

Nicole underwent a long period of learning these new technologies, figuring out how they would work in real time, and understanding their ramifications, and then gave her staff a considerable amount of training time. They tested the system a few tables at a time before going live. The first day or two was a little nerve-racking, with customers entering orders incorrectly, tickets being lost, and hosts not balancing the seating, but everyone soon got the hang of it. After experiencing some bottlenecks in the kitchen when too many people ordered the same dish, they programmed the system to send a message to the tables of customers who ordered backed-up items, alerting them that their meals would require an additional fifteen minutes to prepare.

Customers usually changed their orders, which prevented small delays from escalating. While the usual restaurant disasters occurred from time to time, the systematic process enabled Nicole and her staff to work through these hiccups easily.

The patrons really started to like the system and were happy that it allowed them to enjoy a real sit-down meal without worrying about not getting back to work in time, and word of The Grecian Bank spread quickly through the financial district. When Nicole worked through her early financials, she could see that her investment in innovative processes was, in fact, showing up in her profits. She held a grand opening about a month later, and the operation was as seamless as could be. Even the food critic for the city's leading daily paper gave it a glowing review.

Nicole spent many long hours at the restaurant for the first few months, but after all the kinks had been worked out, things were running so smoothly that she realized that she didn't need to be there all the time. She decided to cut back on her hours and with her newfound spare time, signed up for Weight Watchers and joined a gym to help her lose those extra pounds she'd gained from tasting her own delicious food.

How Chic are You?

↗ HOW MANY CRISES DO YOU HAVE PER WEEK? PER MONTH? EMERGENCIES SHOULD NOT BE THE NORM. CONSISTENT AND RELIABLE PERFORMANCE IS THE BACKBONE OF A GREAT COMPANY.

↗ HOW LONG DOES IT TAKE YOU TO FIND SOMETHING IN YOUR OFFICE? IF YOU SPEND MORE TIME THAN YOU WOULD LIKE TO ADMIT LOOKING FOR THINGS (EITHER PHYSICALLY OR ON YOUR COMPUTER), YOU NEED TO HIRE AN ORGANIZATION CONSULTANT TO GET YOU SORTED.

How much of what you do could be automated? Get everyone producing the highest value they are capable of by automating everything that doesn't require original human thought.

Does everything have a place? Is everything usually in it? Create a process for making this happen automatically.

How many messages do you have in your inbox? What is the date of the oldest email? Learn to take action on things quickly and you will keep moving forward.

Do you understand your own filing system? Can you explain it to others? Investing the time to set things set up in an organized fashion will pay dividends long down the road.

Do people look horrified when they see your place of work? In order for productive things to happen, you need a productive environment. The structure of your business operations should improve, not hinder, the natural flow of work.

Do you have more than three piles sitting on your desk? Do you know what is in them? Ideally, you want to touch each incoming item only once, do what needs to be done (file it, respond to it, or bin it), and get it off your desk. No, putting it in a pile on the floor doesn't count.

Can your competitors do things faster than you can? Speed is a strength of every small business. Get agile. Design fluid processes that can be broken down and put together piecemeal, like Legos, for customization.

CHAPTER EIGHT

Arm's Length or In Bed Together: Strategically Aligning Yourself

Once you start networking for your business, you will meet many people. You'll prefer to keep some at arm's length and get a little closer to others. Just like making friends and exploring the dating scene, all relationships are not created equal. There are different expectations and rewards that go along with having casual acquaintances, lifetime partners, and many other kinds of relationships. A distant, non-integrated relationship remains at arm's-length if you don't invest the time to develop it into something deeper. We all like to feel a sense of connection, and there are clear benefits to cultivating close relationships with the other entities operating in our personal and business environments. At the same time, however, we must remain cautious; getting too close too soon or aligning with the wrong person can cost us dearly. Other people and companies have the capacity to help you and hurt you, so developing the right relationships with the right partners is both a challenge and a great opportunity.

Forming an alliance always involves an element of risk. What if your partner messes up? It happens. We've all heard about the fallout from overzealous outsourcing of manufacturing and service to countries like China and India. While letting go of some elements of your business is a good thing, outsourcing to an unfamiliar entity that you've never met, never seen, and can't really talk to, without setting up the proper parameters can also mean giving up authority and visibility, leaving you vulnerable to quality-control issues. Recalls on children's toys with lead paint on them and dog food laced with harmful chemicals have cost companies millions of dollars. Most of us have also had the pleasure of experiencing outsourced service when we've called up tech support or customer service seeking help, only to reach someone in another country who cannot adequately speak our language and who follows a script that doesn't even address our particular problem. Because of these and other issues, many companies are reconsidering their outsourcing relationships and the effects they have had on customers and are now bringing formerly outsourced activities back in house.

If you tried to do everything you needed or wanted to do inside your company, you would never get it all done. It is inefficient to do everything, especially that in which you are not experienced or educated. It is also expensive. Companies that specialize in one particular area and do a lot of it enjoy those lovely economies of scale I talked about in the last chapter. When they reach this state, they are able to pass along some of their variable cost reduction to their customers. Just like a seasoned tour guide, such companies know the fastest and best way to get their customers where they want to go and how to avoid any potential pitfalls along the way, whereas when rookies try to figure it out on their own, they risk landing themselves and their customers in quicksand. Besides not having the requisite expertise, spending internal time and resources on extraneous tasks can cause you (or others in your organization) to lose focus on your ultimate objective of maximizing the value that your business model adds to the marketplace. This is why outsourcing your non-core competencies can be a winning strategy, but you have to do it right. When you create a mutually beneficial partner arrangement and keep each other informed about timelines, project plans, upcoming opportunities, sales forecasts, and any potential snags you might run into on the way, both partners will benefit and true synergy can take place. This is the goal.

Have you ever ordered a Coke in a restaurant and been told they only served Pepsi? It doesn't happen often here in Atlanta, but this illustrates the essence of partnerships and outsourcing. Restaurants don't want to make their own drinks; they specialize in making food and thus look to beverage companies to create an exclusive arrangement for mutual benefit. Ever notice that Papa John's is the only pizza available at Six Flags? That is also no accident. Many big companies decide to get "in bed together" and develop tight relationships with their partners to the exclusion of competitors. Barnes & Noble and Starbucks show us that marketing partnerships work best when two products go well together. But partnerships are not just for companies that target consumers; they are even more popular, and effective, in business-to-business ventures.

Cisco and Intel are two companies that recognized they could team up and add more value to their customers, as well as benefit each other. Their strategic alliance allows them to improve wireless performance and enhance network security for large enterprises. Their synergistic relationship is rooted in their complementary goals and strengths and has transformed people's lives and the way they do business. Strategic partnerships will help you get more out of everything you do, from your marketing to your innovation efforts. Partners share data, jointly advertise, cross-promote, communicate often, and are always looking for ways to enhance the relationship for mutual benefit. While there are many variations of the concept, all partnerships involve combining the efforts of multiple organizations to improve the results for all involved. In an increasingly global economy, partnering is also a great way to tap into other geographic markets faster and more efficiently than you could on your own.

Whether you call it a partnership, an alliance, or just a friendship, relational capital has value and can help a company get beyond its own four walls, without having to build all of its own roads. Creating strategic alliances with other like-minded and like-marketed companies, and out-sourcing your non-core competencies to subject matter experts, are important steps in building a real company. If you observe how the big guys do it, you'll see that all big companies develop partnerships of one type or another because they recognize the added value these relationships bring. They also understand the importance of maintaining, and not straying from,

> **Chic Tip**
>
> MANAGE YOUR OUTSOURCING RELATIONSHIPS LIKE A PROJECT, WITH A CRITICAL PATH THAT INCLUDES ACTIVITIES THAT BUILD UPON EACH OTHER. TAKE A PROJECT MANAGEMENT CLASS, OR READ A BOOK ON THE TOPIC TO GET FAMILIAR WITH HOW TO THINK IN A PROJECT MINDSET. OUTSOURCING RELATIONSHIPS SHOULD HAVE DEFINED GOALS, DEDICATED RESOURCES, AND A TIMELINE OF STEPS NECESSARY TO ACHIEVE THE DESIRED RESULTS.

their internal strategic focus; they therefore do not want internal resources to work on, much less concentrate on, functions that are not core to their unique value proposition. Partners are a way of gaining leverage and outsourcing is a way to leverage others' manpower and expertise.

As a Chic Entrepreneur, you can't get in bed with everybody (that would not be very ladylike), but I advise that you do get in bed. After playing the field a bit and seeing what is out there, choose a few partnerships in which to invest. Make them strong so they are a win-win for everyone involved, including your customers. There is always an element of risk when taking on partners. Finding the right ones can help you extend your reach and maximize your efficiency. If you haven't already done so, start looking around for complementary people and companies with which you can create lasting relationships.

Beware of Becoming a DIY Entrepreneur

When you build a business as a DIY (do-it-yourself) entrepreneur, the business depends entirely on you, which makes it difficult to break free. As much as you love your company, you need to make sure there is also plenty of time for the other important things in your life. The further down the DIY path that you get, the harder it will be to undo what you've done. Not only should you not try to do everything yourself, you can't. The CEO of the company goes down to the shop floor to oversee the operation, not to implement the new manufacturing techniques. Nor does a CEO spend all of her time in the office working on minutiae; rather, she manages the business by looking at the big picture, demanding performance from each functional area and optimizing how they work together. The CEO sells to big customers, builds relationships with partners, comes up with a marketing strategy, and gets to know the market better. While others are working on the tasks at hand, she oversees operations, innovates, develops new products, and makes the whole business work better. Since the business continues to operate and grow whether the CEO is there or not, she can go to conferences and seminars, spend time with board members and mentors, or just take a vacation. When you build a successful business, this becomes possible.

Outsourcing works on both the macro and micro levels. When your team handles everything outside your personal core competency, you are much better at your piece because you are only doing what you are best at and what you enjoy. Then work becomes fun, which is when your true genius comes out. When you are using your strengths, you are also much more relaxed and confident, and "on." When you impress people with your calm, knowledgeable, and successful demeanor, they will trust you, like you, and want to do business with you. They will also refer others to you. In short, when you partner and outsource, you give yourself room to be the Chicest Entrepreneur you can be.

> **Chic Tip**
>
> STAY ON THE SAME PAGE WITH YOUR OUTSOURCERS—LITERALLY. HAVE TO-DO LISTS AND TIMELINES FOR EVERYTHING THAT NEEDS TO BE DONE. WHETHER YOU EMAIL AN EXCEL SPREADSHEET BACK AND FORTH WITH VENDORS, DISTRIBUTE A CALENDAR, OR UTILIZE WEB-BASED PROJECT MANAGEMENT SOFTWARE, MAKE SURE EVERYONE KNOWS WHO IS SUPPOSED TO DO WHAT AND WHEN, AND MAKE IT EASY FOR THEM TO KEEP UP WITH IT.

In contrast, when you do too much or do things that you are not naturally cut out for, you aren't as good. You risk damaging the level of trust and rapport you have developed with others by appearing less competent, worried, frustrated, frantic, or frazzled. This is why it is important to delegate tasks to people who are better at them than you are. Some business owners get so busy with the operational issues that they lose focus on what is really important. When you are able to focus on the right things, you are much better at what you do and deliver a better quality product and customer and employee experience. Build that strong foundation into your business from the beginning by cultivating good partner and outsourcing relationships, and you'll be poised for explosive growth when the time is right.

A business is not about doing everything from within. It is about finding what you are best at, declaring a core competency, and building a productive backend engine onto that value in order to blast it out to the world. You do this by sourcing materials and hiring a combination of employees and outsourcing partners to create, assemble, and sell end products, and manage the business infrastructure. The end value you create should obviously be greater than the sum of the costs to put it together, but it also needs to be greater than the sum of the end values at each stage of the process. This is how you create a value chain. Your supply chain provides you with the inputs that go into producing your output—whatever you sell for profit—and consists of you, your suppliers, your customers, your outsourcers, and partners. It spans the providers of the basic raw materials that go into what you sell through all of the processes needed to turn them into a finished good. Building a value chain goes beyond mere vendor-of-the-week relationships and linkages that span only one-step of the process of turning inputs into outputs. Instead of making short-term sourcing decisions based primarily on price, value chain participants see the big picture, collaborate on everything from product design to sales and service, and proactively look for ways to increase the value of the end outcome. Each link adds additional and necessary value to the end product. Every time work is handed off from one link in the chain to the next, it must flow smoothly, as if everyone in the chain is on the same team. This chain is vital to the business but should be invisible to the customer, a goal that can be attained by perfecting the seamless handoff. Proper building and management of your value chain comes with learning how to find and work with partners and outsourcers.

Why Outsourcing Makes Sense

Nature operates as a holistic system in which each element plays its respective role: the sun, the rain, the earth, the wind, etc. A plant grows as part of this ecosystem. A plant is not expected to succeed as a system all on its own, and neither is your business. Like a plant, your business also operates in a larger context, and your success comes with the proper utilization of all the elements around you. Outsourcing frees up your time to work smarter and become a better business owner.

With full focus on your strengths, you are able to create the maximum value with your business and thus extract the maximum wealth from it. Once you have a clear understanding of what your true value proposition is, what value you create for the marketplace, and what your focused strategy is for achieving your desired result, you will be able to make the right decisions on what to keep in house and what to outsource. Keen awareness of how your business model works will reveal what your true core competencies are and what are simply supporting activities.

We each have a select and limited number of core competencies. If you are the sole employee of your business, ask yourself, "What am I best at?" If you have a whole company of employees, ask, "What is our true core competency in this business?"

How to Outsource

Interestingly, most people approach the concept of outsourcing with the wrong perspective. Their first thought when they contemplate getting someone else to do something for them is, "How can I get this done the cheapest?" Thinking that way leads a lot of business owners to bad hiring decisions, bad partnerships, poor branding, poor reputation, poor service, poor image (or no image), little customer loyalty, and little insulation from macro and micro economic trends. People who go into an outsourcing decision with this cheapo mentality find themselves perpetually disappointed with performance and results. When companies use cost as their primary motive for outsourcing, they tend to be less satisfied than when they have the intention of actually seeking value or process improvements and the related benefits. Don't let this short-term mentality pervade your thinking or guide your decision-making. Of course, the cash effect is important, but you want to use caution when letting go of anything that could have an adverse effect on your clients, prospects, image, or employees. No one would ever logically expect to be able to create something with the cheapest material available and have it last for years without any problems.

> ### Chic Tip
>
> HIRE A CLEANING PERSON. AS YOU FOCUS ON MAKING YOUR TIME MORE VALUABLE, YOU SHOULD START RIDDING YOURSELF OF TASKS THAT ARE NOT A GOOD USE OF YOUR TIME, SUCH AS CLEANING (YOUR HOME AND OFFICE), OR DOING ANY KIND OF MANUAL LABOR THAT YOU KNOW THE MALE PRESIDENT OF A COMPANY WOULD NEVER DO HIMSELF. GET RID OF TASKS THAT ARE NOT A GOOD USE OF YOUR TIME AND REPLACE THEM WITH MORE OF THE THINGS YOU CAN DO IN THE BUSINESS TO GENERATE CASH. YOU CAN'T SAVE YOUR WAY TO SUCCESS.

Instead of going the cheap route, build a long-term relationship with your outsourced supply chain. Beyond lowering costs, outsourcing decisions need to take into account goals such as improving service levels, streamlining processes, and allowing the internal organization to be more focused on the core value proposition. If cost is still your primary motive, make sure you have two or three other reasons to support this decision, to ensure it is the correct one. Outsourcing done right saves money and increases effectiveness. Done wrong, the opposite effect is likely.

What to Outsource

Given limited resources, you need to be able to focus internally on functions that create the greatest value for the business and for your customers. Outsource the remaining functions that are not part of your core competency and produce little or no value, such as filing, computer repair, bookkeeping, answering the telephone, handling the mail and going to the post office, payroll, taxes, typing, moving, writing, doing research, maintaining your website, sifting through résumés, and managing all of the legalities of human resources. These are all things that must be done, but they do not have to be done by you or anyone within your company.

Building a business is an activity to which the eighty-twenty rule applies: eighty percent of your profits are going to be attributable to twenty percent of your activities. Keep focusing on the small set of activities that yield the highest return and your business will continue to grow.

Chic Caution

AVOID THE USE OF BARTER AS A MEANS OF NOT PAYING FOR SOMETHING, AS IT TENDS TO DEVALUE YOUR VALUE. ONLY WHEN BARTER IS DONE WITH CLOSE FRIENDS AND FAMILY DOES IT SEEM TO WORK. THE MORE DISTANT THE RELATIONSHIP, THE MORE LIKELY IT WILL NOT BE A BALANCED ARRANGEMENT AND THE RELATION-SHIP COULD BE SO STRAINED THAT IT DAMAGES THE OUTPUT. YOU MAY NOT GET EXACTLY WHAT YOU WANT AND FEEL FORCED TO SETTLE BECAUSE YOU DIDN'T PAY, OR YOU MAY END UP GIVING MORE THAN YOUR FAIR SHARE IF THE OTHER PARTY HAS NEVER PAID FOR WHAT YOU PROVIDE OR HAS A DIFFERENT CONCEPT OF WHAT MAKES AN EVEN TRADE.

The Stages of Outsourcing

First, clearly define the task to be outsourced. Let go of the how, focus on the desired end state, and leave it up to the experts to do what they do best. Standardize outsourcing processes and outcomes as much as possible in order to maximize benefits and effectiveness. Develop an RFP (request for proposal). It does not need to be elaborate; maybe it is just one sentence, a paragraph, or a one-page document, but put something down on paper to indicate what you want this outsourcing partner to accomplish for you. Identify whom you will send this to for a quote, what criteria must be met, and what will be the most important factors in your decision-making process (e.g., cost, speed, availability, years in business, prior similar experience, references, organizational culture, values—whatever is most important to your company). Interview a short list of vendors that meet your initial criteria and, if possible and appropriate, use them on a limited basis and assess their performance and your comfort with the relationship before making a more lasting commitment.

Once you select a vendor, make sure the scope of work is meticulously documented, not necessarily in terms of each step, but in terms of outcomes. To mitigate costs, choose an outsourcing provider that will maximize the use of technology; your provider's investment in technology should allow them to reduce their variable costs, which can provide a reduction in price for you. Take into account factors such as their ability to scale to your needs as your company grows and how this arrangement will affect the valuation of your business. It is imperative that you have a rock-solid service level agreement in place that covers how results will be measured, how and how often that information will be furnished to you, and a plan for making any necessary adjustments. While most people are well intentioned, it is always good to put something in writing to keep you both honest. The service level agreement is put in place for the greater good of the relationship.

Outsourcing is used primarily with back-office processes and repetitive tasks with predictable outcomes like data entry, finance (bookkeeping, accounting, and CFO services), HR, legal, administrative, and customer-service call centers; however, during the last decade more companies have started experimenting with outsourcing front-office processes such as research, product design, marketing, and sales. Once you start outsourcing and seeing the benefits, you may not want to stop, but make sure you retain control over what is core to your business value—your true differentiators. Here's an example of how to draw that line. Many companies successfully outsource human resources, because the administrative part is not necessarily vital to their business value. But don't confuse the paperwork side of HR with attracting, retaining, and cultivating talent, because for many companies that is indeed part of their core differentiating value, which they want to keep close to the vest. While you do not want to outsource your strategic strengths, forging and managing good outsourcing relationships can be a strategic advantage and an integral part of how you effectively grow and scale your company to serve your increasing customer base.

Pick the Right Partners
and Execute Properly on the Alliance

It might seem like the simplest thing in the world to join forces with companies whose interests are complementary to yours, but if one or both parties go into the relationship haphazardly, success is less than likely. If inadequate attention is paid to building the relationship and aligning each business's interests and goals to the execution phase, it is doubtful that the relationship will flourish and bear much fruit.

Before you get in bed, make sure

Chic Tip

DROP THE DEAD WEIGHT. IF ONLY TWO OF YOUR FIFTY PARTNERS ARE PRODUCING, DUMP THE DEAD-BEATS AND FIND MORE LIKE THE TWO WORTHWHILE PARTNERSHIPS. QUALITY IS MORE IMPORTANT THAN QUANTITY.

---

you do your due diligence on prospective partners. Ask other companies if they have ever done business with or heard about the company. You also want to partner as high up in the organization as possible. It is nice to trade leads with a sales rep at a company that sells complementary services, but that is not likely to be as effective as if you were to form a relationship with the company's branch manager or CEO. Partnership needs total buy-in from everyone who is to be involved in the legwork, as well as the executive suite. So gain the backing of as many people within the organization as you can. It is also important to understand the expected balance and results of the relationship.

Ask yourself these questions before finalizing a partnership:

- Who is going to put in what?
- How much value should each partner put into the relationship?
- What is the value each partner places on the alliance?
- What does success look like?
- How will we measure how it is going?
- What happens if it doesn't work out?

Both sides do not necessarily have to put in equal value, as long as the ultimate result is of real benefit to both. Similarly, the parties are not necessarily expected to prosper equally from the relationship. This is a partnership designed for mutual benefit, not a competition. Instead of trying to measure who gets more, the real question is, "Are you getting more with this relationship than you would without it?" If so, whether it's equally beneficial or not is irrelevant. More value is always better than no value.

> ### Chic Tip
>
> PARTNER WITH PEOPLE WHO HAVE EQUAL OR GREATER BUSINESS STATUS. HAVING YOUR WEBSITE LINK TO A SHODDY BUSINESS DOES YOUR REPUTATION NO GOOD, BUT IF YOU SURROUND YOURSELF WITH SUCCESSFUL PARTNERS, THEIR PRESTIGE WILL RUB OFF ON YOU.

Partners: Complementary, Supplementary, and Long-term Outsourcing Relationships

Many companies form partnerships for the wrong reason: because it will look good. This is insane. The right reason to form a partnership is to increase sales or decrease costs. Here's a quick litmus test: Will you recalculate your financial projections if the partnership happens? If not, the partnership is probably doomed. You can talk about "visibility," "credibility," and "acceptability" as much as you want, but if you can't quantify the partnership, then you really don't have one.

When you create win-win relationships, you can create a value chain from which your customers can benefit. Many companies use partnerships as a way to team up with other companies that mirror their values and target markets and create greater success for all of the parties involved. As a small business owner, you can overcome feelings of isolation and create great synergies through partnership.

Choose the right partners by asking yourself these questions:

- Are partners committed to both process and outcome?
- Do partners have the capability to make the decisions necessary to move the partnership forward?
- Is there adequate leadership to drive various activities/phases of the partnership?
- Has an adequate assessment been conducted to develop goals and objectives for the relationship?
- Have goals and objectives been articulated adequately to all partners?
- Are goals and objectives agreeable to all partners? Do all partners benefit?
- Are the goals of potential partners compatible with your own mission?

- Have you informed your staff about the relationship?
- Is it worthwhile to define goals through formal agreements or a facilitated process?
- Does the partnership structure assist in defining roles and achieving goals?
- Are there existing models that you can use to structure the relationship appropriately?
- Does the structure of the relationship allow for extension or flexibility in the face of unanticipated changes in the external environment or departure of a partner?
- Are all partners comfortable with the expectations and plans for proceeding?

Some relationships are best kept more transactional in nature. Others are better served by becoming more strategic. Explore which level of intimacy is best for your business objective. Joint ventures are another type of business partnership in which two or more parties embark on a co-owned new enterprise or project and share the risks and the rewards of doing so. Maybe your company has an idea, resources or proprietary technology or intellectual property and could benefit from having the sales or distribution clout of another company. A joint venture requires the same type of strategic planning, management, and leadership as an entirely new business, so be sure to formalize this type of relationship.

You can expand your reach substantially by partnering with a larger company that has national or global distribution capabilities. By staying informed about the larger business context around you, you can identify areas where there might be an opportunity for your firm to fit in. Maybe a large retailer is trying to better penetrate the senior citizen market, and you've just developed a product that would help the retailer do that. Develop a target list of larger companies that would be good partners for you, research those companies and put together a sales pitch to sell them on what you would be able to do for them. Be sure to be realistic about your aspirations; many big companies won't even talk to you until you are a certain size, and they will only be interested if you can add substantial value to them. As global markets open up and competition grows, small to midsize companies need to be increasingly creative about how and with whom they align themselves, and what benefits they expect to get from doing so. Balance the risks and rewards of forming tight alliances.

Some potential benefits of global partnerships:

- Offering your customers a larger variety of products or services
- Spending less time and money developing new products
- Increasing the size of your sales force, yet only adding to variable costs
- Sharing advertising and marketing costs
- Offering existing customers more coverage geographically or longer support hours
- Gaining additional skilled resources
- Increasing the total number of existing customers to whom you can sell the next generation of your products and services
- Adding credibility to your business and earning the trust of potential customers
- Expanding your business more rapidly, or developing new products and services faster
- Solving your customers' problems faster
- Learning ways to improve customer service
- Benefiting from having more strategic thinkers on your team

- All of these will make you more competitive in the domestic and global marketplace.

Negotiating the Terms of the Partnership

Once you are ready to partner, you must decide who gets what. The whole idea here is to create more value and wealth, so you need to outline what the rewards are to each party when the desired results are achieved. In a partnership, this usually means sharing revenue that results from a joint initiative or receiving a referral bonus of a flat dollar amount or a percentage of sales revenue earned. When you outsource, offering incentives for work completed on time and surpassing expectations is an inexpensive way to develop relationships and ensure you always get the best performance. Don't worry that paying for these incentives will take money out of your pocket; you'll find the amount you have to "give away" is far less than what you receive, making it a good ROI.

As relationships progress and deepen, you are apt to face the question, "Shall we become exclusive?" Clearly, outsourcing and partner acquaintances differ from outsourcing and partner marriages. There is only so far an uncommitted relationship can go. Outsourcing can be more intimate than a typical supplier relationship; it is common to share confidential information such as demand forecasting, upcoming innovations, or R&D projects to make your outsourcing arrangement a win-win partnership for the long term. Just how exclusive you want to be will depend on the nature of your strategic partnerships. If it seems like a fair and even trade and you are not leaving a big opportunity cost on the table by cutting off your ability to partner with others, perhaps that's a good arrangement to lock in. However, if you feel that committing to just one partner in a particular area would be too limiting, don't tie yourself down. You could also outline boundaries, by declaring that the arrangement is exclusive "in this geographic region" or "in this one product or service line," so you are not bound to send your partner everything that falls remotely under their umbrella.

Once you've decided if you are going steady or not, your next question is, "Shall we make this contractual or keep it informal?" If you are sure about this relationship and decide upon exclusivity or if money is changing hands, I would absolutely recommend putting it in writing. One of your important trusted allies should be a good attorney, who can help you clearly define the specific parameters of your relationships.

Once you get the partnership going, don't wait too long before you recognize early success in the relationship. Identify short- and medium-term objectives, and look for small accomplishments to celebrate and build momentum upon them. Make sure both partners are taking every opportunity to promote the partnership within their own communities and networks. Consider sending out a joint press release to tell the rest of the world.

Chic Tip

PLACING RECIPROCAL LINKS TO EACH OTHER'S WEBSITES WILL HELP INCREASE YOUR SEARCH ENGINE RANKINGS, AND THOSE OF YOUR PARTNERS.

Here are some questions to assist you in monitoring the results of your alliances:

- Are the accountability requirements of all partners met?
- Is a financial system in place to measure accountability requirements?
- What are the criteria for success? Are they linked to annual goals and objectives?
- Are partners collectively responsible for both decisions and results?
- Are the timeframes for achieving success specified and reasonable?

- Are there resources dedicated to measuring outcomes?
- Are there agreements in place as to how public communications will be handled?
- Is the relationship seamless to the customer?
- Who should communicate with the customer? How and how often?

Meet Pauline and Patricia

Pauline and Patricia are two small business owners who integrated outsourcing and partnering into their business models. Pauline is a life coach whose business, Life Visions, needed a website. When she first started her business, she created her own simple website with only four pages of basic content that explained her mission and her services. However, as her business grew and her own insights into her business and her customers' needs increased, she decided that she needed a website that looked as professional as she was and matched the logo and branded stationary a graphic designer had created for her.

Pauline had found the graphic designer easily enough; he was a friend of her next-door neighbor. Chad had a full-time job, but was always looking for extra design work and had created the logo, business cards, note cards, and letterhead for Pauline. She was proud of these printed materials and wanted to be equally proud to send clients and prospects to her website. Chad had been very easy to work with, and when Pauline told him about wanting an updated website, Chad promised to create a customized logo to fit the format of her new website.

Over the year that they worked together, Chad sent Pauline two client referrals and she referred other business owners to him. Pauline knew from experience that knowing someone made doing business with them easier. She also knew that she couldn't create this next version of her website on her own, but neither could she afford a top web designer to develop and maintain her website. Pauline began asking around for a recommendation. Days later at a networking event, Pauline was introduced to Billy, and they immediately hit it off. They discovered they went to the same college and shared some inside jokes. Billy told Pauline about the custom software development company he owned and how he integrated backend systems like accounting and inventory management with a web-based reporting application. When Pauline heard the words "development" and "web," she told him that she needed a website developed for under $5,000. Billy admitted that he didn't normally do website development, but that he had developed his own website and had the web design software and a server and could therefore develop and maintain Pauline's new site.

In a meeting to discuss the details, Pauline was impressed to see that Billy could use Flash Player to put animation and videos on websites, and she thought his website looked good. Billy told Pauline that he could capture contact information of visitors interested in receiving a newsletter and her web traffic statistics. Even though Pauline didn't have a newsletter, because writing wasn't her strong suit, and she didn't know how she would use the statistics, she liked the idea that Billy could provide these things for her. Billy also informed Pauline that she would have to provide the verbiage for the website, but promised her that he could work within her $5,000 budget. Pauline was relieved that he could accommodate her budget, and agreed to his terms and signed a contract the following week.

Billy suggested that Pauline look over other websites and send him an email with links to what she liked and why. They exchanged a few emails back and forth to clarify the color scheme and layout. As Billy built the website, Pauline started writing the web content in a Word document. She used her existing website as a starting point, and specified what content should go where on the new site. When Pauline was finished, she emailed the document and the customized logo Chad had created to Billy, feeling satisfied that outsourcing this work had gone smoothly.

Billy emailed back to say that the content Pauline had written didn't fit into all of the website content blocks, and suggested that they meet again so he could show her how to maintain her website content. Pauline was confused by this turn of events, since she had assumed that Billy would "maintain" it for her, as he had said. When they met, Billy explained that maintaining the website meant that he would keep it on his server, not log into the site and make content changes. He showed Pauline this in their contract, and told her she would have to make her content fit the website and update it whenever she wanted. Billy added that he would do any backend development that she needed in the future for a nominal fee, but reiterated that he did not manage content.

Pauline couldn't believe that she hadn't understood this in the beginning. She sat through the hour-long tutorial on how to use the website that Billy developed, and went home to input her content. It took Pauline weeks of fiddling with the website to get the content the way she wanted it. When she accidentally deleted whole boxes of content, she had to call Billy to walk her through the correct way to upload and save changes.

When Pauline finally finished her website, she emailed friends and family to take a look at it and give her any comments or suggestions. Pauline received several emails telling her about typos, some people told her that they couldn't tell what she did by the look of the website, and others suggested that she change the fonts and images. A friend who worked in marketing commented that the navigation from page to page wasn't intuitive—the pages didn't flow naturally from one to another, and told her there was no call to action and that her website was just an online brochure. Frustrated, Pauline spent more time fixing the typos and trying to decide how to make her website flow better, look more like that of a life coach, and provide more value so people would want to call her.

Plugging away at her website, Pauline lost countless hours she could have used to drum up new business. When she was with clients, she was so tired from staying up late staring at the computer the night before that she could hardly concentrate. When she finally finished, Pauline was not thrilled with the look of the website and was angry with herself for not being more thorough when specifying what she needed Billy to do. To top it off, Pauline met a web designer at a networking event three months later who said he could develop a sophisticated website and have a copywriter do the content all for under $4,000. Even though this debacle was Pauline's own fault, she was glad that she didn't run into Billy ever again, because if he'd been at arm's length, she would have wrung his neck.

Now meet Patricia. Patricia is a calligrapher. She started her business, Pen Strokes, in her spare time while she worked as an accountant. Patricia was doing enough business to make a profit every month, but knew that in order to be successful she needed partners to spread the word about her business to her target market: women throwing parties.

Patricia decided to target women's networking groups and social clubs in order to seek out potential partners: event planners, florists, caterers, and cake makers. When she had networked and asked for referrals in the past, most people never got back to her with an actual referral. She wanted to make sure that she created partner arrangements that would work, so she developed an incentive arrangement. When Patricia met potential partners, she asked them to coffee, where she made a formal presentation about her business not just a request for referrals. Then she presented them with a business proposition that would allow each to profit. Patricia would give a fifteen percent discount that the potential partner could mark up. Patricia asked each potential partner to make the arrangement a win-win by offering her an incentive

> ### Chic Tip
>
> GET NOTE CARDS PRINTED AS PART OF YOUR CORPORATE STATIONERY, AND SEND PERSONAL CARDS TO EVERYONE THAT YOU MEET FOR LUNCH AND COFFEE TO DISCUSS BUSINESS SYNERGIES OR OTHERWISE SHARE A GOOD CONNECTION. THERE IS NOTHING MORE SINCERE AND MEMORABLE THAN A HANDWRITTEN NOTE. IT ONLY TAKES A FEW MINUTES; IF PRINCESS DIANA COULD FIND THE TIME TO DO IT, SO CAN YOU.

for referring clients their way, and most were happy to offer her some sort of referral bonus.

Patricia and the partners that she began working with also agreed to put links on each other's websites and keep each other's business cards to give out. When Patricia had lined up a sizeable amount of partners, she started meeting with them regionally. For instance, in one section of town, where she knew an event planner, a florist, and a caterer, she got them all together and proposed jointly hosting a seminar called "How To Become the Hostess with the Mostest." At the seminar, each partner would present a brief, informative, and entertaining talk and field questions from the audience. Complimentary food and beverages would be provided, along with information on each partner.

After the latest seminar, Patricia got a call from Joyce, an event planner she'd recently started working with, who said, "Patricia, my company is putting on an exhibition at next year's bridal expo. Now that we're in bed together, I was hoping that you could do the calligraphy for our invitations."

What can we learn
from Pauline and Patricia?

Pauline failed to research her options properly before outsourcing part of her business and ended up with most of the work dumped right back into her own lap. She did not have experience working with website developers, so she should have written down all of her expectations for design, content, and maintenance first, and then interviewed a variety of candidates to hear suggestions from the experts and determine what her options (including costs) were. Many small business owners make the mistake of trusting the first nice person they meet at a networking event and taking the easy way out, instead of doing the necessary research. It is nice to like your partners, but it is more important that they have the experience and expertise necessary to do what you need. Ideally, you can find both, but don't sacrifice competence for camaraderie.

Patricia, on the other hand, looked for partners strategically. When she found the right partners, she presented them with a business proposition that was too good for them to refuse or forget about. Going forward, Patricia continued to deepen and enhance her relationships with her partners by organizing seminars with them.

As a Chic Entrepreneur, you must develop long-term business alliances with companies that will grow with you. Don't gouge your outsourcers on price; be a good client to them so they can grow their business and serve yours. Expand your reach with partners you can stand on the shoulders of, and then share the view with them so that you both can gain. When choosing partners, ask if they are the right strategic fit for your long-term plan. Make sure your visions are aligned early in order to save yourself the trouble and heartache of an ill-fitted relationship. Once you find the right fit, spoon.

How Chic are You?

⬧ ARE YOUR PARTNERSHIPS MUTUALLY BENEFICIAL? ASKING WITHOUT GIVING IS RUDE AND GIVING WITHOUT GETTING IS ALLOWING OTHERS TO BE RUDE.

⬧ WHEN YOU PARTNER WITH SOMEONE, IS IT WITH THE INTENTION OF INCREASING THE VALUE YOU ARE CREATING FOR EACH OTHER'S CLIENTS OR FOR BOTH BUSINESSES' BOTTOM LINES? YOUR INTENTION NEEDS TO CONTAIN A LITTLE BIT OF BOTH.

⬧ HOW MANY FORMALIZED PARTNERSHIPS DO YOU HAVE? DON'T LET YOUR FEAR OF COMMITMENT LEAVE YOU STANDING ALONE IN THE CORNER. YOU'LL DANCE MORE IF YOU PARTNER UP.

⬧ WHEN WAS THE LAST TIME YOU SAW/TALKED TO/WENT TO LUNCH WITH EACH OF YOUR PARTNERS? CONTINUALLY MANAGE YOUR PARTNER RELATIONSHIPS BY ATTENDING TO THEM BOTH PROFESSIONALLY AND PERSONALLY.

⬧ DO YOUR PARTNERS EACH HAVE A DOCUMENT THAT EXPLICITLY OUTLINES THE EXPECTATIONS YOU HAVE FOR THEM? YOU CAN'T EXPECT PEOPLE TO DO WHAT YOU WANT THEM TO IF YOU NEVER TELL THEM EXACTLY WHAT THAT IS. MAKE SURE EACH OF YOUR PARTNERS KNOWS HOW TO BE A GOOD PARTNER TO YOU.

⬧ WOULD YOU RECOMMEND YOUR OUTSOURCERS TO OTHERS? ONCE YOU'VE OFFLOADED A TASK TO SOMEONE ELSE, IT IS EASY TO BECOME COMPLACENT. DON'T MAKE DO WITH MEDIOCRE OUTSOURCING. DEMAND THE QUALITY THAT YOU EXPECTED WHEN YOU ENTERED INTO THE ARRANGEMENT OR END IT. DON'T LET OTHERS GET AWAY WITH NOT SATISFYING YOU.

CHAPTER NINE

Webvan or Amazon:
Have a Plan and Measure Your Results

Grocery shopping can be a nightmare in many big cities. If you've ever lived in an urban area, you know what it's like to walk three blocks to where your car is parked on the street (hopefully it's not raining), drive to a grocery store, pick out your goods, carry them out to your car, load up, drive home, park three blocks from your apartment, and then haul your bags up four flights of stairs, where you fumble with your keys as the bag with eggs and tomatoes smashes to the ground just before you push open your door.

Consequently, you would think that a company like Webvan would have made it. I know there have been plenty of times I would have gladly paid a premium to order groceries online and have them delivered. Webvan was an online grocery delivery business that went bankrupt in 2001. Imagine having someone bring all of your groceries to your doorstep, even that one artichoke you need for dinner, a tube of your hard-to-find brand of toothpaste, a pint of Ben and Jerry's, and fresh flowers. This seemingly brilliant concept failed because the company didn't adequately plan for consumer preferences and measure consumer demand. Webvan began by purchasing an excess of vans, food, and warehouse facilities before getting the sales to afford them. They drove around empty vans to try to start a buzz and make consumers think that *everyone else* was buying from Webvan so they would follow suit. However, demand took longer to ramp up than anticipated, as consumer-shopping habits take time to change, and Webvan wasn't paying enough attention to metrics to notice this and adjust. Because of this measurement oversight, and the push to rapidly build its infrastructure, overhead far exceeded sales and eventually investors pulled the plug, forcing Webvan to close up shop. While the company certainly was offering unique value, the market timing wasn't right and the concept didn't catch on.

Amazon could have gone down in flames just like Webvan did. However, because of the initial strategic plan (that did not anticipate a profit for four to five years) and subsequent slow growth, Amazon was able to stave off bankruptcy when the dotcom bubble burst. Amazon also did something unique by making personal suggestions to shoppers. While other online and brick and mortar retailers were just measuring growth and suggesting their top sellers to everyone, Amazon used data mining techniques to measure and analyze the purchases of individual consumers and then used behavioral targeting to offer other items that might appeal to that particular customer. The company used a predictive model to leverage sales data in a more intelligent way than simply measuring sales results. This data became intellectual property that could be used to bring in even more revenue. By expanding offerings over time, building up globally, and really utilizing consumer information, Amazon created an online revolution in a market that saw so many other dotcoms bomb.

Everyone knows that you are supposed to have a business plan when you start a business, yet the majority of small businesses are started without one. The goal of this chapter is not to tell you how to write a business plan; plenty of books have been written on that topic and I suggest browsing that section of your local bookstore (or Amazon) and adding one of the good ones to your library. Instead, we are going to explore the value behind the exercise of planning and discuss how to make planning and measurement a permanent part of how your organization operates, so you can use planning in your business to make you more agile and adaptive to continuous evolution.

Failing to Plan Is Planning to Fail

Planning is essentially goal setting, and goal setting has been proven to be one of the most effective ways to achieve anything. Without a plan, you are just winging it and have little hope of actually creating anything more than a job for you and perhaps a few others, none of which will be secure. Have a plan. Make it a good one. Be an Amazon.

As a Chic Entrepreneur, your business plan will serve as a map to help you navigate along the journey that your business will take. You do not need a picture-perfect, textbook business plan. Who can write one of those the first time? And what good is it to anyone if it sits on the shelf collecting dust? The format and appearance are less important than the activity itself. Going through the mental exercise of planning and producing some kind of written document will help you think through different possibilities and decide on the best path to get where you want to go. It will also help you to think through contingencies so that when something unexpected happens, you already have considered the alternates and can make a decision easily.

The plan must be written down and include a description of the business, the need you are filling, the market you are in, what you sell, and how you will sell it, along with who your competition is and how you are different, who's on your team, how you operate internally, and your financial forecast. It must also include strategies, tactics, and numbers, along with the resources you have and how you will use them to achieve the goals you are setting. Everything you do in your business will require resources, and resources will always be limited, so consider resource allocation when you are creating your plan. There are plenty of great business plan templates out there, so there's no need to start from scratch. Find an outline and start filling it in.

The degree of formality of your plan depends upon its intended audience and use. Is this to be an internal or external document? Unless you need it for a specific purpose, like getting someone to lend you money, a formal business plan can be a time sink that keeps you from other more important priorities, so a less formal plan will often work better. The more succinct it is, the more likely you are to refer to it and use it as a guide.

Start with Where You Are Today

Imagine someone calling you up and asking you for directions to your house. Your first question would be, "Where are you coming from?" If the answer is, "I don't know," chances are this person is never going to make it to your house. In order to get somewhere, you must know your starting point.

Start with an initial benchmark of where your business is today in each of the key areas below:

- Sales
- Fixed costs
- Variable costs

- Profit
- Revenue growth percentage (month–to–month and year–to–year)
- Profit growth percentage (month–to–month and year–to–year)
- Customers
- Average revenue per customer
- Average order size or sale
- Customer retention rate
- Employee retention rate

Next, set your goals in each area for a reasonable period—I would start with one year. Create an action plan of how to close the gap between your current state and the desired future state. The plan is your map, and tactics and action are what will get you to your desired destination. Progress by definition must involve some form of measurement, so measure your performance against your starting benchmark to track your progress. Identify areas that need attention and make necessary adjustments to keep you on track so you can achieve your desired results.

Many people do not clearly set goals for their business. They instead decide to "see what happens." This passive attitude shows not only laziness, but also a failure to understand the principles of the universe in which you are operating. You create "what happens," so if you don't make things happen, little will. Once you know where you are today and where you want to go, you can identify successful strategies that will take you toward your goals.

Resource Requirements

Anything you don't prioritize and assign responsibility for is unlikely to happen amid the hustle and bustle of running a business. Therefore, you need an operational plan of action at the end of your business plan to help you follow through. The operational plan is a timeline of what needs to happen and when. This is not to be confused with an operating plan that you would include in a formal business plan to explain how you do what you do, your facilities, hours of operations, etc. Your operational plan of action outlines activities outside of normal day-to-day operations that will move your strategic plan forward to reach your goals. Since it is usually easiest to break it out by month, list the next twelve months and bullet what you plan to accomplish during each one.

Here's an example of what this might look like:

January

- Hire new technician
- Train technician on all core job responsibilities
- Cross-train on customer service
- Complete sketches of new product designs chosen at board meeting

February

- Meet with manufacturer to design a prototype
- Send press release
- Refresh web content with new product info
- Lunch with top two strategic partners to discuss expanding distribution

Put these on your calendar's to-do list so that there's no chance you'll accidentally forget to accomplish these items. Time flies when you own a business, and before you know it, it will be this time next year.

What Are the Most Critical Numbers in Your Business?

Key metrics will allow you to monitor your company's performance. You must identify a way to measure performance so that you can determine at a glance what you are doing well and what you are doing poorly. Your metrics will give you an indication of where you or your managers need to focus attention. Think of this as your executive dashboard, similar to your car's dashboard, that you can look at as you drive your company forward. This will give you an overall view of how your organization is running and alert you to any issues that require attention. Your dashboard will consist of a handful of key metrics that act as a constant health check, a way for you to check the business's pulse and other vital signs. Metrics are great and powerful tools, and as you get more comfortable with them you will learn to use them to spot opportunities and more effectively manage your business. Put your current and desired future states into numbers. More customers, less turnover, increase revenue, improve operations, and lower costs are not goals. Collect data and start developing a culture of measurement, because you can only improve what you measure. Sophisticated business reporting is now accessible to businesses of any size, allowing them to get a snapshot of their business in terms of all of their key metrics. Aside from the big ones like revenue, profits, and the percentage of growth of these numbers, what numbers do you need to manage,

> ### Chic Tip
>
> COME UP WITH A THEME FOR EACH YEAR. AS YOUR STRATEGY UNFOLDS AND EVOLVES, YOU'LL HAVE BUILDING YEARS WHERE YOU STRENGTHEN YOUR FOUNDATION AND EXPANSION YEARS WHERE YOU SPREAD YOUR WINGS. YOU MAY HAVE LEAN AND MEAN YEARS WHERE YOU NEED TO CUT COSTS AND GET AS EFFICIENT AS POSSIBLE. THEMES CAN ALSO INCLUDE THINGS LIKE COMMUNITY OUTREACH, EDUCATION, TEAMWORK, LEADERSHIP, AND CREATIVITY.

make decisions, and track the progress of your company? Metrics remove the subjectivity from the business and give you hard data to look at in order to make better decisions.

Some other metrics that may be useful for you to keep an eye on are:

- Sales close rate
- Time it takes to perform critical business tasks
- Defect rates
- Returns or rework
- Cost of capital
- Return on investment of anything you are spending money on
- Advertising response rates
- Employee productivity rates in terms of output, sales, or service
- Customer satisfaction ratings
- Number of referrals and their sources

Some metrics should be analyzed together. For instance, it is good to look at cost of customer acquisition in combination with the lifetime value of a customer and customer retention rate, and some measure of renewals or repeat business can be analyzed in conjunction with average sales per customer, for forecasting and business valuation.

Obviously, there are a lot more metrics to calculate, and each business has a unique set of key performance indicators. It is your job to find the ones that provide you with the best insight into what is really going on within your company. Don't pick ones that are vaguely interesting; pick metrics that are driving your business. As the business grows, each position and department will also have key metrics that fall under their control. You need to make sure that the right information gets to the right people in a timely manner and in a format they can understand, analyze, and use to make decisions. New reporting capabilities, such as dashboards, scorecards, and an array of graphical displays of data, from pie charts and bar graphs to gauges and heat maps, are available and affordable and make it easy to see what is going on. It is relatively easy to put data into most applications, but getting it out is another story, so when you go to purchase software or have an application designed for your business, look at both the ease of inputting data and the usefulness of the output. Remember that clarity is power when you are structuring your knowledge-management and business-intelligence capabilities. Keep your data-collection process clean and as automated as possible, and systematize how often and the way in which metrics are provided.

You also want to communicate your critical business metrics to employees. When they understand how the business runs and what can make it better, they will be more vigilant in finding ways to help. Show your team that you are serious about holding people accountable to these numbers by rewarding employees whose efforts improve the stats. Perhaps your team deserves a bonus when a certain goal

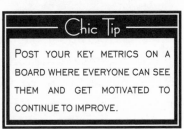

Chic Tip

POST YOUR KEY METRICS ON A BOARD WHERE EVERYONE CAN SEE THEM AND GET MOTIVATED TO CONTINUE TO IMPROVE.

is met. If it has, let them know and keep track of their progress, so they can celebrate and be rewarded when they hit it. Information is only valuable when it is used to do smart things, so now that you have created a way to get good data, use it to make good decisions. Your measurement effort needs to be purposeful and motivate the "right" behaviors. Your metrics should not be cumbersome or difficult to decipher, but objective and immediately actionable.

You Can Only Improve What You Measure

Businesses are created from the inside out, but they must be monitored from the outside in. While nearly all business owners

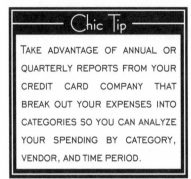

observe metrics at some level, most use them like a rearview mirror, judging performance after it has happened and thinking of measurement in the past tense. Additionally, people tend to err in one of two extremes in their use of metrics. Either they don't measure anything

at all and essentially run their business with a metric blindfold on, or they measure every little thing, drown themselves in details, and fail to see the big picture. Be a Goldilocks and find the happy medium of getting just the right amount of information.

Chic Entrepreneurs know that a culture of continuous improvement is vital for business success. It shows your customers that you care about having long-term relationships with them, rewards the desired attitude and behavior in employees, and allows you to continue to grow, which is essential. Businesses are living entities. They must always be growing, or else they are dying. They can never just stay the same. Continuous improvement means growth.

Spending More Time on Your Business
Will Allow You to Spend Less Time in It

Once they have used metrics to examine their businesses, many owners conclude that they should do less, not more. A Chic Entrepreneur does not try to do a million different things; instead, she sets up a framework where everyone in the organization has a clearly defined role, and she determines key metrics for the desired output of each function. Ideally, you, as the owner of the business, do not factor into the metrics at all. You want to be working *on* your business, not *in* it. Thus, you want your business to be so efficient that you are completely taken out of all equations. That way, you might one day be able to take a vacation for a month to a desert island with no Wi-Fi while your business runs as effectively as ever without you.

Before you remove yourself entirely from the equation, the value of your time has a direct correlation to the amount of personal wealth you will amass, and the value you can extract from each hour of everyone who works for you has a direct correlation to the value of your business. To tackle this concept, let's take a look at High ROI Time vs. Low ROI Time. High ROI (or productive) Time is time spent generating revenue and streams of passive income, or improving employee performance in high-impact areas. Productive time is time spent selling; increasing the value of existing

> **Chic Tip**
>
> KNOW THE EXPECTED RETURN ON THE INVESTMENT OF EVERY NEW INITIATIVE YOU SPEND TIME AND MONEY ON. BEFORE YOU BEGIN A NEW PROJECT, HAVE CLEAR GOALS IN MIND AND DETERMINE HOW YOU WILL MEASURE YOUR PROGRESS. DON'T WAIT MONTHS TO ASSESS HOW IT IS WORKING. AS SOON AS YOU GET SOME DATA, START MAKING IT BETTER.

products and services; creating new products; improving your sales or marketing process; inspiring, training, or delegating to others so they can take on more of your responsibilities; setting up joint-venture deals; and creating economies of scale and leverage in your business. On the other hand, time spent sitting in traffic or on hold listening to Muzak is Low ROI Time.

For an activity to be productive, it must be both efficiently performed and effectively executed. Efficiency and effectiveness are two sides of the same coin and the two dimensions you must balance when you look at how performance is assessed and improved. The percentage of time that most people spend in either of these categories is staggeringly low. Studies done on Fortune 500 CEOs estimated they had only twenty-eight to thirty-eight minutes of productive time per day. However, as a small business owner, you have some advantage over a corporation CEO, because you are closer to your business and have less to oversee. Increasing your productive time requires discipline and focus, but it is necessary if you want to cultivate an enjoyable role for yourself that allows you to get the most out of your desired lifestyle, as well as experience the joys of business achievement. The more valuable you can make your time, the less time you'll have to put in, and the ultimate goal of any Chic Entrepreneur is to work less, instead of more, while earning more in the process.

A Planning Exercise

To see where you are spending your time, color-code all of your activities by highlighting each in a different color, either on your paper or electronic calendar. See what colors dominate your week or month. Make a list of all of your different activity categories, as well as how much each activity category yielded that week or that month. Divide the time spent by the dollar yield, and you'll have a value of dollars per hour for each activity. Rank your activities from highest yield to lowest yield and look at the top ten. Figure out how much money per hour you could make if you were to fill your weeks just doing those activities. Set that as your new minimum standard hourly rate. Next, go back through all of the other activities that you performed during the week and determine the hourly rate or total cost for which you could outsource each one. Start with the ones that you can outsource for the least money and keep moving up the list. Spend each extra hour you free up doing more of your five highest-yield activities. Spend more time doing the things you love, are best at, and yield the greatest hourly rate of return on your time.

Your Time Also Represents
Your Personal Power

Not to get too mystical, but we all have only a limited amount of personal power or life-force energy at our disposal. There are ways to maximize yours, but ultimately there is a finite limit to how many hours are in a day, a week, and a year, and how much focus, concentration, and energy you have to give. To create a successful and fulfilling life, you must make wise decisions about how and where you will dedicate your precious time and energy. Measure the ROI on everything you do to advance the business, including physical, emotional, and mental efforts. It is okay to give, give, give to the business at the beginning, but you must continue to measure the ROI of all of this giving, because your time

> ### Chic Tip
> STAY CURRENT. IF YOUR BUSINESS WERE TO BE IN A REALITY TV SHOW, WHICH ONE WOULD IT BE? HOW ABOUT A TALK SHOW OR NEWS PROGRAM? LOOK TO CURRENT EVENTS AND INTO THE FUTURE AND ASSESS HOW TRENDS SUCH AS GOING GREEN, NEW TECHNOLOGY, GLOBALIZATION, AND SOCIAL NETWORKING COULD AFFECT YOUR BUSINESS AND THINK OF WAYS YOU CAN TAKE ADVANTAGE OF THESE TRENDS.

really is not supposed to be a gift to the business. You see, a gift is something that you give and expect nothing in return, but when give your time and emotional energy to the business, you should expect something in return. Remember, that is the whole point: Resources going in should produce value coming out. That is how this business thing is supposed to work. Expect a profit from everything you do. Respect your time, your personal power, and your mental and physical energy. Notice where it is invested and how it is recharged. As the Chic Boss, you must cultivate self-awareness to know what you need in addition to what your customers and employees need.

Last but not Least: Passing the Baton

Another thing to plan for is your graceful exit, otherwise known as succession planning. The founder of a business has the clearest understanding of what made the company successful. However, the competitive landscape will change over time, and the new leaders must be capable of applying the lessons of the past to the new world in which they now compete. When you are preparing to step down off your Chic Empress throne, you need to groom a successor who will allow the company to continue its necessary evolution in a way that keeps it close to the initial strategy that made it successful in the first place. What would your successor need to know, have, or be like?

Meet Yu and Yolanda

Let's look at how Yu and Yolanda, two small business owners, used planning and measuring in their businesses.

Yolanda owns a property flipping business called Yo Houses. While working as a paralegal at a law firm, she bought a foreclosure property, put some money into repairing it, and went over on weekends to do small projects. A few months later, she sold it for a $30,000 profit. Yolanda was so excited by her success and the idea of owning her own business that she quit her job at the law firm to flip houses full time.

Soon Yolanda bought two more houses and sold them both for a handsome profit that enabled her to bring on two part-time employees to help with the growing administrative headache of paperwork.

Yolanda had a formula that was simple: She found houses that needed mainly cosmetic work, avoiding those that required structural repairs. She did all the painting herself, inside and out, and updated each home's carpeting, lighting, kitchen, and bathrooms. Yolanda worked largely by intuition. When she found a house on which she felt she could make a profit, she purchased it. Yolanda did her business's marketing like a lot of others in her industry: She used the Internet, purchased two billboards, and put signs at heavily trafficked intersections. Yolanda's business was going strong, and she was consistently buying and flipping houses, making a profit on each.

There were two equally important sides to Yolanda's business—finding property and finding buyers. Therefore, Yolanda had to direct her various marketing efforts to two separate audiences. Yolanda's formula for fixing houses was carefully planned, but she did not keep a tally of the profitability of each marketing effort. Capturing the effectiveness of those efforts could have helped her adjust her marketing mix, reducing or increasing techniques as necessary.

Unfortunately, the business kept Yolanda so busy that she never had time to read the paper or watch the news, so she was taken completely aback when the housing market in her area took a hit. It just so happened that Yolanda had been on her most aggressive purchasing spree ever and at that point owned ten houses that she had intended to flip in the next six months. She had put work into five of the houses already and her monthly loan payments totaled $15,000. Because Yolanda hadn't planned for a real-estate slump, she didn't have the money to pay all the mortgages for more than two months, unless she sold something. She took a loss on the houses she could sell; and after losing the other two to foreclosure, her business went bankrupt. Contemplating selling her car to pay off her debts, Yolanda wished Webvan was still around to deliver her groceries.

Now meet Yu. Yu was always an avid gym rat and when she got the opportunity to buy her own gym, she jumped at the chance. She named her gym Sweat Spot and worked hard to make the gym as progressive as possible, with updated machines and certified personal trainers on staff. Yu also installed a swipe card system, with readers at the front desk and both side entrances, so that she could monitor members coming and going and determine peak hours through printed reports showing how many people were in the gym at any given time. This automation also eliminated the need for a staff member to sit at all the entrances, keeping her team lean and productive. Her gym's computer system also kept track of all of the members' information, did automatic credit card billing, and if an exception kicked out, the system automatically sent an email reminding people to pay on time to avoid a lapse in membership.

Yu was pleased with how her membership was expanding and she kept adding amenities, such as dispensers with conditioning shampoo and liquid soap in each shower stall and a supply of emergency toiletries in case someone forgot something. Instead of keeping fresh towels on hand, she gave all members a plush towel with their first names sewn on and offered a laundry service; she had run the numbers and determined that this approach would reduce water and electricity use substantially, and then asked her members for their opinions and found that they liked the idea.

One day, Yu started chatting with a tired gym member, Ted. Ted told Yu that he had worked late all week and was so out of it he couldn't even remember what exercises he should do at the gym. He commented, "I wish someone would just keep track of my workouts and remind me what to do so I wouldn't end up doing arms four times a week. That way I could just come here and go on autopilot and wind down, and not worry about what exercises I'm supposed to be doing, or if I'm going to wind up all disproportional. It would also be great if I could track my own progress."

Yu asked Ted why he didn't use a trainer and he replied that scheduling with a trainer was too restrictive because he didn't always know when he would have time to come in, and he added that when he came in after work, he liked to work out alone to relieve stress. Yu asked him why he didn't put his workout information in an organizer or a calendar. Ted said that he did use the calendar on his phone occasionally, but that he would frequently forget to do it.

That night, Yu started wondering if there was a solution to Ted's problem, and if there were other members who faced and were frustrated by this same challenge. Knowing that most of her customer base worked full time, she guessed that more members probably had the same issues. Yu began talking to her associates and searching the Internet to find a solution. That was how she found out about Fitrix™, a new software that would keep a record of a person's body metrics like current weight, resting and active heart rate, percentage of body fat, and body-mass index, and maintained their workout schedule and emailed them reminders about future workouts.

Yu scheduled a consultation with a Fitrix representative and with his help, calculated an expected return on the investment in the software; she found that it would pay for itself within a year. Certified personal trainers were expensive, so Yu always wanted to maximize their billable hours and reduce their administrative time and any time spent not with a client. Fitrix would allow her to increase the productivity of her personal trainers by fifty percent. She also anticipated that it would provide a competitive advantage that would increase her membership without having to pay for additional advertising, as her happy customers would likely spread the word about the revolutionary system. After learning about the capabilities and costs, Yu ran the numbers with her accountant and determined that she could afford to buy the software for Sweat Spot the next quarter.

Four kiosks were installed on the Sweat Spot workout floor. Members could read short tutorial brochures on how to use the system. After inputting their body metrics and workout preferences, members received workout reminders via email. Members could use the computers at the gym or login from their own computers to update their body metrics and change their workout preferences in Fitrix.

Yu wanted to make sure that her members were using and benefiting from the system, so she placed customer satisfaction cards by the kiosks. She showed incoming members how to use the system and used it as a selling point when she was giving a prospective member a tour. She also hosted appreciation parties where members who used Fitrix were recognized for their results, diligence, and consistency, and given little prizes for their progress. This became quite a motivational experience and led the entire gym community to become more cohesive. Members started to bond and make friends with each other. Yu's metrics revealed that member dropout rates had declined, and new member rates were increasing. The overwhelming response was that Fitrix was a hit and the reason that many members stayed with Sweat Spot and told more of their friends about it.

After using the system for six months, Ted came to Yu and said, "Using Fitrix has made my life so much easier. This system makes working out as easy as buying stuff from Amazon." That year, Sweat Spot was named the city's best private gym by two different newspapers.

How Chic are You?

↗ Do you know what you are going to do every day, or do you just show up at work and see what happens? Write out the next day's must do's and can do's every night before you leave the office or go to bed, or first thing each morning. You'll stay on task and be less vulnerable to distraction by tangential concerns.

↗ How many metrics have you defined to measure success? Who measures them and how often?

↗ When people ask you how business is going, are you sure you know the answer? Answering "Things are great," is a good reflex response, but you'll feel a lot better about saying it when you really feel it, and the only way to do that is to know where you've been, know where you are going, know how the ride has been, and know what you can expect in the future.

↗ How often do you look at your financial statements? Monthly? Quarterly? Annually? Use them as a management tool to proactively take your business forward, rather than simply as a record of what happened in the past.

↗ Do you know how effective your last marketing campaign really was? Every marketing effort can be measured by its success in terms of dollars invested to dollars yielded. Intangible value (such as name recognition) can also contribute to the success score, if and only if you feel it will eventually pay dividends.

↗ When was the last time you celebrated one of your successes? When you measure, you know when it's time to revel in the glory of your

ACHIEVEMENT. BUILDING CELEBRATION INTO THE WORK CULTURE WILL MOTIVATE YOUR TEAM AND MAKE GOING TO WORK A HECK OF A LOT MORE FUN AND PURPOSEFUL FOR EVERYONE.

DO YOU KNOW WHAT YOU WANT YOUR BUSINESS TO LOOK LIKE IN FIVE YEARS? HOW MANY PEOPLE WILL YOU HAVE? WHAT WILL ANNUAL REVENUES BE? WHAT WILL YOUR ROLE BE IN THE COMPANY?

CHAPTER TEN

The Chic Message

Most entrepreneurs fail because they quit. They are not one hundred percent committed, so when things get tough, they decide to get out. They glance through employment postings and fantasize about someone offering them a dream job that they just wouldn't be able to turn down, or they have delusions of an investor or buyer purchasing their floundering business even though it is not of any value. Instead of putting their hearts and souls into the business at hand and risking it all for success, they tuck their tails between their legs, scurry off the entrepreneurial field, and play on somebody else's turf.

Entrepreneurship is hard. It will test you like you have never been tested before, and you will fail repeatedly. You will feel disappointed, confused, and overwhelmed, and you will be tempted to give up and follow an easier path.

Many new entrepreneurs I meet have been laid off, were dissatisfied with their jobs, or decided to follow their passion, and they tell me, "I decided to give entrepreneurship a try." People think being your own boss is easy, so they enter entrepreneurship unprepared and then are not willing to continue to challenge themselves, to keep learning, growing, getting better, and pushing through their fear and uncertainty.

Entrepreneurship is not something you try; it is something you must commit to in order to be successful. Women tend to be eager to commit to relationships, to marriage, to their families, and even to their best friends, but when it comes to committing to business, ironically, women are the ones who can't commit.

My intention in writing this book is to show you that you can be a Chic Entrepreneur. You have what it takes to make a business work. It starts with a seed of vision, which will blossom and grow when you make the right decisions. The power is within you; you just have to do what it takes to put it all together. Owning a business requires self-reliance, and becoming self-reliant is one of the greatest gifts you can give yourself. However, you also need to be humble enough to ask for help when you need it. Your business may be all yours, but that doesn't mean you have to do it all by yourself. If your intentions are honorable, people will want to help you succeed, so let them. Having a strong desire is important, but just wanting something to happen will not make it so. You must dare to dream, and then dare to do.

Before you can let out that sigh of relief, there will be struggles. Business ownership is not as glamorous as it's cracked up to be. You don't declare yourself an entrepreneur and instantly morph into Donald Trump or Oprah Winfrey. They didn't start where they are now, either. Getting a business off the ground is hard work, but hard work builds character, and if you stay true to yourself and your integrity along the way, you will like the person that you morph into even better.

Those who have committed to their dream business keep

going. They keep moving forward, remaining undeterred and positive even when the worst has happened, knowing in their hearts that they will find a way to make their business succeed. This is the commitment I'm talking about. Most people do not have it, so despite having books, training seminars, the Small Business Administration, coaches, and consultants available, when push comes to shove, they don't stand up to the challenge, and they quit. Once you accept and take ownership of your decision to become a Chic Entrepreneur, you will know in your heart that you can get over any hurdle that gets in your way. By mastering the nine key elements of every successful business that I've laid out for you in this book, you can make it happen.

I've worked long and hard to build my business. It's my passion and I'm proud of everything I've accomplished and struggled through these last ten years. I wish that same feeling of satisfaction for a risk well taken on every woman who desires to pursue entre-preneurship, in addition to the joy, pride, and financial and personal freedom that comes with business success. Along my journey to create a consulting firm, I realized that I needed a methodology to use as a guiding model with which to teach and impart wisdom to my clients and to awaken their own business genius, as well as to differentiate my firm from the many other business consultants and coaches littering a crowded marketplace. That's when I came up with the Flourishing Business Methodology, which is a pictorial outline of what every business needs to implement to be successful. While it is possible to have a business without each of these nine dimensions, to have a flourishing business, you must create and continually improve upon these nine elements. This book is based on that methodology and focused specifically on applying it to female entrepreneurs who desire Chic Success.

The Flourishing Business® Methodology

Most successful people have had the opportunity to accept failure at some point (often numerous times) in their lives, but they have realized that it is failure only if you let it make you fail. They are committed to succeeding, so they keep going, and eventually they do achieve success. That is the lesson that every entrepreneur needs to learn in order to be successful.

Starting your own business has been touted as the path to wealth creation, but this is only true if you can turn your business into an asset that works without you. A flourishing business is a business that is managed and run by other people and does not require your physical presence. If it is necessary that you do all, most, or even some of the work, you merely own your own job, not a flourishing business.

Entrepreneurship is not for everyone. Have the presence of mind to know what you are getting yourself into, and be wise enough to walk away if you recognize that business ownership is not for you, or that your current venture is not going to work. Don't empty your purse of all you have before you come to that realization. There are other ways to create wealth if this is not your bag, but they too require money in order to make money. Judicious risk management means: Don't bet the farm, bet the barn.

Having assets that produce cash flow and appreciate is the real path to wealth. This path can be traveled using the vehicle of business or through other means such as stocks, bonds, and real estate. In order to get your assets to work for you, you must be able and willing to take care of and nurture them with all they need to produce and grow. Therefore, whatever types of assets you chose, you need to love and understand them.

If you do decide to pursue entrepreneurship, do so with fearless gusto, tireless determination, and impassioned and intelligent optimism. Realize that it will not be easy, that you will have to overcome many setbacks and obstacles, and that you can't give up the first time something doesn't work out—or the twentieth time, for that matter. There will be many ups and downs on this emotional rollercoaster ride, which is why it is important to celebrate your victories when you have them. Although you may never cease wanting more, you must remember to give thanks for what you have today. Learn to manage your state as best you can. Self-discipline is one of the most powerful tools you have. Take control of your life and commit to your mental and physical health as well as to the success of your company. Structure your life's priorities around your values, and realize that if success in business is important to you, you must make it a priority.

I meet people every day who tell me they have always wanted to start their own business. I tell them, "If income is all you're after, there are plenty of easier ways to make a living, but building a business can be one of the most gratifying and fulfilling things you accomplish in your lifetime." Decide if you are really willing to commit to making it happen.

There have been numerous setbacks in my own pursuit to build a real business, even embarrassing, infuriating, and heartbreaking ones that made me wish I could quit. But something deep inside wouldn't let me. I was compelled to push on. And just when I thought I might never see the sun, the dawn began to break. Fate tests our commitment, but it is through the setbacks, the failures, and the adversity that we become strong enough to deserve our success.

I wish you a comfortable pair of shoes for your journey and a purse full of profits.

Stay Chic!
Elizabeth W. Gordon

The following are some of the resources
that we provide for those who are interested
in upping their Chic Quotient
during and after reading this book.

Chic Information

Visit our website
www.chicentrepreneur.com
to sign up to receive more
Chic Tips **for building your** Chic Empire

Chic Camaraderie

Chat with other entrepreneurs on our
Chic Chat Blog.
Communicate knowledge,
cultivate relationships, celebrate success.

Chic Style

Purchase items and accessories to help you act and look the part.

Other Great Business Books for the Entrepreneurial Woman

Call in your order for fast service and quantity discounts!
(541) 347- 9882
OR order on-line at www.rdrpublishers.com using PayPal.
OR order by mail: Make a copy of this form; enclose payment information:
Robert D. Reed Publishers
1380 Face Rock Drive, Bandon, OR 97411
Note: Shipping is $3.50 1st book + $1 for each additional book.

Send indicated books to:

Name: _____

Address: _____

City: _____ State: _____ Zip: _____

Phone: _____ Fax: _____ Cell: _____

E-Mail: _____

Payment by check   ☐ or credit card   ☐   (All major credit cards are accepted)

Name on card: _____

Card Number: _____

Exp. Date: _____ Last 3-Digit number on back of card: _____

	<u>Qty</u>
The Chic Entrepreneur	
by Elizabeth Gordon ....$12.95 _____	
Ten Commitments for Women	
by Susanne Blake .... $11.95 _____	
100 Ways to Create Wealth	
by Steve Chandler & Sam Beckford .... $24.95 _____	
Who's Hiding in Your Address Book?	
by Mary Kurek .... $12.95 _____	
How Bad Do You Really Want It?	
by Tom Massey ....$19.95 _____	
The Joy of Selling	
bu Steve Chandler..$11.95 _____	
Ten Commitments for Building High Performance Teams	
by Tom Massey .... $11.95 _____	

Quantity: _____ Amount: _____

+ Postage: _____

Total Amount: _____

*Visit **www.rdpublishing.com** for more great titles!*